"This series is a tremendous resource for those wanting to study and teach the Bible with an understanding of how the gospel is woven throughout Scripture. Here are gospel-minded pastors and scholars doing gospel business from all the Scriptures. This is a biblical and theological feast preparing God's people to apply the entire Bible to all of life with heart and mind wholly committed to Christ's priorities."

BRYAN CHAPELL, President Emeritus, Covenant Theological Seminary; Senior Pastor, Grace Presbyterian Church, Peoria, Illinois

"Mark Twain may have smiled when he wrote to a friend, 'I didn't have time to write you a short letter, so I wrote you a long letter.' But the truth of Twain's remark remains serious and universal, because well-reasoned, compact writing requires extra time and extra hard work. And this is what we have in the Crossway Bible study series *Knowing the Bible*. The skilled authors and notable editors provide the contours of each book of the Bible as well as the grand theological themes that bind them together as one Book. Here, in a 12-week format, are carefully wrought studies that will ignite the mind and the heart."

R. KENT HUGHES, Visiting Professor of Practical Theology, Westminster Theological Seminary

"*Knowing the Bible* brings together a gifted team of Bible teachers to produce a high-quality series of study guides. The coordinated focus of these materials is unique: biblical content, provocative questions, systematic theology, practical application, and the gospel story of God's grace presented all the way through Scripture."

PHILIP G. RYKEN, President, Wheaton College

"These *Knowing the Bible* volumes provide a significant and very welcome variation on the general run of inductive Bible studies. This series provides substantial instruction, as well as teaching through the very questions that are asked. *Knowing the Bible* then goes even further by showing how any given text links with the gospel, the whole Bible, and the formation of theology. I heartily endorse this orientation of individual books to the whole Bible and the gospel, and I applaud the demonstration that sound theology was not something invented later by Christians, but is right there in the pages of Scripture."

GRAEME L. GOLDSWORTHY, former lecturer, Moore Theological College; author, *According to Plan, Gospel and Kingdom, The Gospel in Revelation,* and *Gospel and Wisdom*

"What a gift to earnest, Bible-loving, Bible-searching believers! The organization and structure of the Bible study format presented through the *Knowing the Bible* series is so well conceived. Students of the Word are led to understand the content of passages through perceptive, guided questions, and they are given rich insights and application all along the way in the brief but illuminating sections that conclude each study. What potential growth in depth and breadth of understanding these studies offer! One can only pray that vast numbers of believers will discover more of God and the beauty of his Word through these rich studies."

BRUCE A. WARE, Professor of Christian Theology, The Southern Baptist Theological Seminary

T0335307

KNOWING THE BIBLE

J. I. Packer, Theological Editor
Dane C. Ortlund, Series Editor
Lane T. Dennis, Executive Editor

•   •   •   •   •   •

Genesis	Psalms	Jonah, Micah, and Nahum	Ephesians
Exodus	Proverbs		Philippians
Leviticus	Ecclesiastes	Haggai, Zechariah, and Malachi	Colossians and Philemon
Numbers	Song of Solomon		
Deuteronomy	Isaiah	Matthew	1–2 Thessalonians
Joshua	Jeremiah	Mark	1–2 Timothy and Titus
Judges	Lamentations, Habakkuk, and Zephaniah	Luke	
Ruth and Esther		John	Hebrews
1–2 Samuel	Ezekiel	Acts	James
1–2 Kings	Daniel	Romans	1–2 Peter and Jude
1–2 Chronicles	Hosea	1 Corinthians	1–3 John
Ezra and Nehemiah	Joel, Amos, and Obadiah	2 Corinthians	Revelation
Job		Galatians	

•   •   •   •   •   •

J. I. PACKER was the former Board of Governors' Professor of Theology at Regent College (Vancouver, BC). Dr. Packer earned his DPhil at the University of Oxford. He is known and loved worldwide as the author of the best-selling book *Knowing God*, as well as many other titles on theology and the Christian life. He served as the General Editor of the ESV Bible and as the Theological Editor for the *ESV Study Bible*.

LANE T. DENNIS is CEO of Crossway, a not-for-profit publishing ministry. Dr. Dennis earned his PhD from Northwestern University. He is Chair of the ESV Bible Translation Oversight Committee and Executive Editor of the *ESV Study Bible*.

DANE C. ORTLUND (PhD, Wheaton College) serves as senior pastor of Naperville Presbyterian Church in Naperville, Illinois. He is an editor for the Knowing the Bible series and the Short Studies in Biblical Theology series, and is the author of several books, including *Gentle and Lowly: The Heart of Christ for Sinners and Sufferers*.

JEREMIAH

A 12-WEEK STUDY

Matthew S. Harmon

:: CROSSWAY®

WHEATON, ILLINOIS

Knowing the Bible: Jeremiah, A 12-Week Study

Copyright © 2016 by Crossway

Published by Crossway
          1300 Crescent Street
          Wheaton, Illinois 60187

All rights reserved. No part of this publication may be reproduced, stored in a retrieval system, or transmitted in any form by any means, electronic, mechanical, photocopy, recording, or otherwise, without the prior permission of the publisher, except as provided for by USA copyright law. Crossway® is a registered trademark in the United States of America.

Some content used in this study guide has been adapted from the *ESV Study Bible*, copyright © 2008 by Crossway, pages 1363–1474. Used by permission. All rights reserved.

Cover design: Simplicated Studio

First printing 2016

Printed in the United States of America

Scripture quotations are from the ESV® Bible (The Holy Bible, English Standard Version®), copyright © 2001 by Crossway, a publishing ministry of Good News Publishers. Used by permission. All rights reserved.

Trade paperback ISBN: 978-1-4335-4908-3
EPub ISBN: 978-1-4335-4911-3
PDF ISBN: 978-1-4335-4909-0
Mobipocket ISBN: 978-1-4335-4910-6

Crossway is a publishing ministry of Good News Publishers.

VP		31	30	29	28	27	26	25	24
15	14	13	12	11	10	9	8	7	6

TABLE OF CONTENTS

SERIES PREFACE

KNOWING THE BIBLE, as the series title indicates, was created to help readers know and understand the meaning, the message, and the God of the Bible. Each volume in the series consists of 12 units that progressively take the reader through a clear, concise study of that book of the Bible. In this way, any given volume can fruitfully be used in a 12-week format either in group study, such as in a church-based context, or in individual study. Of course, these 12 studies could be completed in fewer or more than 12 weeks, as convenient, depending on the context in which they are used.

Each study unit gives an overview of the text at hand before digging into it with a series of questions for reflection or discussion. The unit then concludes by highlighting the gospel of grace in each passage ("Gospel Glimpses"), identifying whole-Bible themes that occur in the passage ("Whole-Bible Connections"), and pinpointing Christian doctrines that are affirmed in the passage ("Theological Soundings").

The final component to each unit is a section for reflecting on personal and practical implications from the passage at hand. The layout provides space for recording responses to the questions proposed, and we think readers need to do this to get the full benefit of the exercise. The series also includes definitions of key words. These definitions are indicated by a note number in the text and are found at the end of each chapter.

Lastly, for help in understanding the Bible in this deeper way, we would urge the reader to use the ESV Bible and the *ESV Study Bible*, which are available online at esv.org. The *Knowing the Bible* series is also available online.

May the Lord greatly bless your study as you seek to know him through knowing his Word.

J. I. Packer
Lane T. Dennis

WEEK 1: OVERVIEW

▲

Jeremiah was born into a priestly family and raised in the small town of Anathoth (1:1), located in the tribal allotment of Benjamin, a few miles north-east of Jerusalem. God called him to be a prophet while still a young man, in 627 BC (1:2, 6), and set him "over nations and over kingdoms, to pluck up and to break down, to destroy and to overthrow, to build and to plant" (1:10). His repeated calls for repentance and his criticism of Judah's kings led to a life of significant persecution. Yet for more than 40 years Jeremiah spoke the word of God to the southern kingdom of Judah as it ran headlong toward God's judgment of exile[1] in 587/586 BC.

God's condemnation of Judah's idolatry takes place on the stage of world history. The Babylonians were God's instrument of judgment on Judah for repeatedly breaking the covenant[2] (21:8–10), but they too must pay for their wickedness (50:1–51:64). None of the surrounding nations will escape the Lord's judgment on all the earth (46:1–49:39). Yet those who turn from their sins and trust in the Lord will be saved, Jew and Gentile alike (3:6–4:4).

God's message through Jeremiah, however, was not one solely of judgment, but of hope as well. In fact, the bleakness of Judah's sin sets the backdrop for the beauty of God's promised salvation through a righteous Branch from the line of David who will not only reign in righteousness but will *be* our righteousness

(23:5–6). Days will come when God will make a new covenant in which he will forgive sin and write his law on the hearts of his people (31:31–34).

Jeremiah shows us that the Lord truly abounds in steadfast love and faithfulness, while at the same time he remains perfectly just by punishing sin (compare Ex. 34:6–7). Through judgment God will save a faithful remnant and establish a new covenant with them through a descendant of David. (For further background, see the ESV *Study Bible*, pages 1363–1368; available online at esv.org.)

▶ Placing It in the Larger Story

Jeremiah served during a significant transition in salvation history. Although his ministry began during the reign of the last faithful king (Josiah), he eventually saw God fulfill his long-standing promise of judgment on Judah for its covenant unfaithfulness. But it was during these dark days that God promised not only to bring a remnant back to the land but also to institute a new covenant through a faithful Davidic king. These promises find their fulfillment in Jesus Christ, the Son of David who established a new covenant through his death and resurrection.

▶ Key Passage

"Behold, the days are coming, declares the LORD, when I will make a new covenant with the house of Israel and the house of Judah, not like the covenant that I made with their fathers on the day when I took them by the hand to bring them out of the land of Egypt, my covenant that they broke, though I was their husband, declares the LORD. For this is the covenant that I will make with the house of Israel after those days, declares the LORD: I will put my law within them, and I will write it on their hearts. And I will be their God, and they shall be my people. And no longer shall each one teach his neighbor and each his brother, saying, 'Know the LORD,' for they shall all know me, from the least of them to the greatest, declares the LORD. For I will forgive their iniquity, and I will remember their sin no more." (Jer. 31:31–34)

▶ Date and Historical Background

Jeremiah's ministry spanned more than 40 years, from his call to be a prophet in 627 BC through the destruction of Jerusalem in 587 and extending into the early years of the exile. His scribe Baruch recorded Jeremiah's messages and prophecies, likely compiled in their final form by 550 BC. King Josiah (640–609 BC), the last faithful king, instituted a number of reforms, but they were not enough to turn Judah from the path of destruction. Caught in the power struggle between Egypt and Babylon, Judah struggled to maintain its independence. In 605 BC Babylon took the first wave of exiles (including Daniel and his friends; Dan. 1:1–7), and deported a second group in 597 (including Ezekiel; Ezek. 1:1–3). The final straw came in 587/586 BC, when Nebuchadnezzar laid siege to Jerusalem, destroyed the city and its temple, and took a large number of exiles back to Babylon. Jeremiah was among those left in Jerusalem. But when a group of Judeans killed the Babylonian-appointed governor, Gedaliah, those responsible fled to Egypt, taking Jeremiah and Baruch with them against their will. Jeremiah continued his prophetic ministry there, prophesying against the sins of Judah, Egypt, Babylon, and other nations, and presumably he died there as well.

Outline

I. Introduction (1:1–19)
    A. Jeremiah's historical setting (1:1–3)
    B. Jeremiah's call and message (1:4–16)
    C. God's promised protection of Jeremiah (1:17–19)

II. Israel's Covenantal Adultery (2:1–6:30)
    A. Israel as a faithless spouse (2:1–3:5)
    B. Israel's need to repent (3:6–4:4)
    C. The coming disaster (4:5–31)
    D. Judah's unwillingness to repent and its consequences (5:1–31)
    E. God's rejection of his people (6:1–30)

III. False Religion and an Idolatrous People (7:1–10:25)
    A. Judah's improper reliance on the temple (7:1–8:3)
    B. Judah rejects God's Torah (8:4–17)
    C. Judah's deceit (8:18–9:9)
    D. Jeremiah's grief (9:10–26)
    E. Judah's idolatry (10:1–16)
    F. Judah's future exile (10:17–25)

IV. Jeremiah's Struggles with God and Judah (11:1–20:18)
    A. Jeremiah's surprise (11:1–12:17)
    B. Jeremiah's lament (13:1–15:21)
    C. Jeremiah's renewal (16:1–17:18)
    D. Jeremiah's burden (17:19–18:23)
    E. Jeremiah's suffering (19:1–20:18)

V. Jeremiah's Confrontations (21:1–29:32)

    A. Judah's kings (21:1–23:8)

    B. False prophets (23:9–40)

    C. Judah's people (24:1–25:38)

    D. False belief (26:1–29:32)

VI. Restoration for Judah and Israel (30:1–33:26)

    A. Restoration (30:1–24)

    B. New covenant (31:1–40)

    C. Return to the Promised Land (32:1–44)

    D. Davidic covenant (33:1–26)

VII. God's Judgment on Judah (34:1–45:5)

    A. God's faithfulness and Judah's infidelity (34:1–35:19)

    B. Rejection of God's word (36:1–32)

    C. Jerusalem's last days (37:1–39:18)

    D. Judah's futile rebellion against Babylon (40:1–41:18)

    E. Judah's futile rebellion against God (42:1–45:5)

VIII. God's Judgment on the Nations (46:1–51:64)

    A. Egypt (46:1–28)

    B. Philistia (47:1–7)

    C. Moab (48:1–47)

    D. Many nations (49:1–39)

    E. Babylon (50:1–51:64)

IX. Conclusion: The Fall of Jerusalem (52:1–34)

    A. Jerusalem's fall and Zedekiah's blinding (52:1–11)

    B. Destruction of the temple (52:12–23)

    C. Exiling of the people (52:24–30)

    D. Continuation of the Davidic lineage (52:31–34)

As You Get Started

Based on your current understanding of Jeremiah, what are some of its key themes? Are there particular passages or verses that come to mind when you think about the book?

Take some time to read through 2 Kings 22–25, which records events during the lifetime of Jeremiah. Write down some observations about key events, the leaders of Judah, and its people.

What aspects of Jeremiah are you most looking forward to studying? Are there any specific questions that you hope to have answered through this study?

As You Finish This Unit . . .

Take a few minutes to ask God to bless you with increased understanding and a transformed heart and life as you begin this study of Jeremiah.

Definitions

[1] **Exile** – Several relocations of large groups of Israelites/Jews have occurred throughout history, but "the exile" typically refers to the Babylonian exile, that is, Nebuchadnezzar's relocation of residents of the southern kingdom of Judah to Babylon in 586 BC (residents of the northern kingdom of Israel had been resettled by Assyria in 722 BC). After Babylon came under Persian rule, several waves of Jewish exiles returned and repopulated Judah.

[2] **Covenant** – A binding agreement between two parties, typically involving a formal statement of their relationship, a list of stipulations and obligations for both parties, a list of witnesses to the agreement, and a list of curses for unfaithfulness and blessings for faithfulness to the agreement.

WEEK 2: INTRODUCTION

Jeremiah 1:1–19

▲

The Place of the Passage

This opening chapter introduces us to the prophet Jeremiah and foreshadows his ministry. After the historical stage is set (1:1–3), God calls Jeremiah to be his prophet to the nations (vv. 4–16). By putting his words in Jeremiah's mouth, God appoints him "over nations and over kingdoms, to pluck up and to break down, to destroy and to overthrow, to build and to plant" (v. 10). Fulfilling this ministry will cause Jeremiah great suffering, but God promises to protect him (vv. 17–19).

The Big Picture

Jeremiah 1:1–19 shows Jeremiah's commission to speak God's words of judgment and restoration to Judah and the nations.

Reflection and Discussion

Read through the complete passage for this study, Jeremiah 1:1–19. Then review the questions below concerning this introductory section to Jeremiah and write your notes on them. (For further background, see the *ESV Study Bible*, pages 1369–1371; available online at esv.org.)

1. Jeremiah's Historical Setting (1:1–3)

Like many other prophetic books, Jeremiah begins with a list of kings who reigned during his 40-year ministry. Josiah (640–609 BC) was the last good king of Judah, instituting a number of reforms (2 Kings 23:1–25). Jeremiah was called in the thirteenth year of Josiah's reign (627 BC); according to 2 Chronicles 34:1–7, what reforms had Josiah begun the year before? Based on Jeremiah 1:13–16, what should we conclude about the effectiveness of these reforms?

2. Jeremiah's Call and Message (1:4–16)

God begins his call to Jeremiah by saying, "Before I formed you in the womb I knew you, and before you were born I consecrated you" (1:5). Why do you think God begins in this way? What effect do you think these words would have had on Jeremiah?

Jeremiah initially responds to God's call by protesting, "Ah, Lord GOD! Behold, I do not know how to speak, for I am only a youth" (1:6). Like Moses (Ex. 3:1–4:16) and Solomon (1 Kings 3:5–9) before him, Jeremiah was overwhelmed by God's call. How does God reassure him (Jer. 1:9)?

After reassuring Jeremiah in verses 7–8, "the LORD put out his hand and touched" the prophet's mouth (v. 9). God did a similar thing when calling the prophet Isaiah (Isa. 6:1–7). In Isaiah this act symbolizes God's cleansing Isaiah of his sin. What does this act symbolize here in Jeremiah?

According to Jeremiah 1:10, God calls Jeremiah "to pluck up and to break down, to destroy and to overthrow, to build and to plant." Look up how these same word pairs are used in 18:7–11; 31:27–30; and 45:1–4. Based on these passages, what do these phrases mean?

In 1:11, God shows Jeremiah an almond (Heb. *shaqed*) branch, then in verse 12 he tells him, "I am watching over [Heb. *shoqed*] my word to perform it." As the first tree to bud in the spring, the almond tree was said to "watch for spring."

What does the imagery of the almond branch tell us about God's commitment to his word and to Jeremiah his prophet? How would this reassure Jeremiah?

God shows Jeremiah a second vision, that of a "boiling pot, facing away from the north" (1:13). The boiling pot symbolizes "the tribes of the kingdom of the north" (i.e., Babylon) who will surround the cities of Judah, including Jerusalem (vv. 14–15). Why is God allowing this? What has Judah done to provoke God's judgment?

3. God's Promised Protection of Jeremiah (1:17–19)

God acknowledges that Jeremiah's commission is a difficult one. What four commands does the Lord give Jeremiah (1:17)? What is the meaning of the imagery of verse 18? What is the relationship between God's command to Jeremiah and what God promises to "make" him?

Jeremiah's commission to speak the words God puts in his mouth will not make him popular. According to 1:18–19, who will oppose Jeremiah? What two things does God promise Jeremiah in response?

Read through the following three sections on *Gospel Glimpses*, *Whole-Bible Connections*, and *Theological Soundings*. Then take time to consider the *Personal Implications* these sections may have for you.

Gospel Glimpses

GOD DELIVERS HIS PEOPLE. Just as the Lord promised to deliver Jeremiah from his many enemies (Jer. 1:8, 19), so too Jesus Christ delivers us from our greatest enemies—sin, death, and the Devil. Through his death and resurrection, Jesus has freed us from our sins (Rom. 6:1–11), removed the sting of death (1 Cor. 15:51–57), and crushed the head of the great serpent, Satan (Gen. 3:15; Luke 4:1–13; Col. 2:15). God's promise of deliverance sustained Jeremiah amid his suffering. How much more should we draw encouragement from what God has done for us in Jesus amid our own suffering?

GOD'S PLANS ENCOMPASS THE NATIONS. God did not raise up Jeremiah as a prophet merely for Judah; instead he appointed him "over nations and over kingdoms" (Jer. 1:5, 10). God promised to bless all the nations of the earth through Abraham (Gen. 12:1–3), and that promise finds its fulfillment in Jesus Christ. He is the promised descendant of Abraham who received the inheritance and shares it with all who are united to him by faith, regardless of their ethnicity (Gal. 3:6–29). Through his redeemed people God will take the gospel to the ends of the earth (Matt. 28:18–20).

Whole-Bible Connections

CAPTIVITY. Captivity, or exile, is a prominent form of judgment in the Bible. When Adam and Eve sinned, they were exiled from the garden of Eden (Gen.

3:22–24). Because of their persistent and unrepentant idolatry, the northern kingdom of Israel was sent into exile by the Assyrians in 722 BC (2 Kings 17:1–41). Jeremiah prophesied and lived to see the same fate befall Judah at the hands of the Babylonians (Jer. 52:1–30). Through his death on the cross, Jesus experienced the exile from God that we deserved because of our sins (Heb. 13:12). But in this fallen world we remain "sojourners and exiles" (1 Pet. 2:11), awaiting the day when "the dwelling place of God is with man. He will dwell with them, and they will be his people, and God himself will be with them as their God" in a new heaven and earth (Rev. 21:3).

KNOWN BEFORE BEING FORMED IN THE WOMB. God's first words to Jeremiah were, "Before I formed you in the womb I knew you, and before you were born I consecrated you" (Jer. 1:5). In the mystery of his sovereign will God ordains people to specific roles in his redemptive plan before they are even born—Isaac as the promised descendant of Abraham and Sarah (Gen. 17:15–21); older brother Esau serving his younger brother Jacob (Gen. 25:19–27); Samson delivering the Israelites from the Philistines (Judg. 13:1–5); Isaiah's servant of the Lord redeeming Israel and being a light to the nations (Isa. 49:1–6); John the Baptist preparing the way for Jesus Christ (Luke 1:5–17); Jesus as the one who would save his people from their sins (Matt. 1:18–25); and Paul as the apostle to the Gentiles (Gal. 1:15–17).

Theological Soundings

THE WORD OF GOD. The word of the Lord is something that comes to Jeremiah, not something he produces on his own. While God has revealed himself in a general way through creation itself (Ps. 19:1–6; Rom. 1:19–23), only in his word do we find a complete witness to who God is, what he has done, who we are as human beings, how we can know him, how we should live, and the true nature of the world around us. God's word is the means by which he accomplishes his purposes, whether it is creating (Gen. 1:1–31) and governing the world (Jer. 1:9–10) or calling his people to participate in his mission (Matt. 28:18–20). The ultimate expression of the word of God is Jesus Christ, who took on flesh to dwell among us (John 1:14–18). God has given us the Bible as the written Word of God so that we may know him and live in a way that pleases him (2 Tim. 3:14–17).

IDOLATRY.[1] God judges Judah because they have forsaken him and worshiped other gods (Jer. 1:16). Idolatry is often subtle, taking something that is itself good (e.g., family, ministry, relationships, and work) and making it our ultimate goal or passion. Anything or anyone we put before the Lord in our lives is an idol, since God alone deserves our worship and devotion (Ex. 20:1–6; Deut. 6:4–6; Matt. 22:37–40). Those who worship idols begin to resemble them

(Ps. 115:4–8); likewise, as we worship the true God we increasingly become like him (2 Cor. 3:18).

Personal Implications

Take time to reflect on the implications of Jeremiah 1:1–19 for your own life today. Consider what you have learned that might lead you to praise God, repent of sin, and trust in his gracious promises. Make notes below on the personal implications for your walk with the Lord of the (1) *Gospel Glimpses*, (2) *Whole-Bible Connections*, (3) *Theological Soundings*, and (4) this passage as a whole.

1. Gospel Glimpses

2. Whole-Bible Connections

3. Theological Soundings

4. Jeremiah 1:1–19

> ### As You Finish This Unit . . .

Take a moment now to ask for the Lord's blessing and help as you continue in this study of Jeremiah. And take a moment also to look back through this unit of study, to reflect on some key things the Lord may be teaching you—and perhaps to highlight and underline these things to review again in the future.

Definition

[1] **Idolatry** – In the Bible, usually refers to the worship of a physical object. Paul's comments in Colossians 3:5, however, suggest that idolatry can include covetousness, since it is essentially equivalent to worshiping material things.

Week 3: Israel's Covenantal Adultery

Jeremiah 2:1–6:30

▲

The Place of the Passage

This section contains a series of five messages describing how Israel broke her covenant with the Lord. Israel is an adulterous wife who has pursued other gods (Jer. 2:1–3:5), and God is calling her to repent (3:6–4:4) because disaster is coming (4:5–31). Judah's stubborn refusal to repent will bring serious consequences (5:1–31) and result in God rejecting his people (6:1–30). Throughout this section God reminds Israel of his particular love for her—he is Israel's husband who redeemed her out of slavery in Egypt and entered into an exclusive covenant with her. Such extraordinary grace makes Israel's unfaithfulness all the more shocking.

The Big Picture

Jeremiah 2:1–6:30 vividly describes Judah's persistent idolatry as spiritual adultery that violates Yahweh's[1] covenant with them.

Reflection and Discussion

Read through the entire text for this study, Jeremiah 2:1–6:30. Then interact with the following questions and record your notes on them concerning this section of Jeremiah's prophecy. (For further background, see the *ESV Study Bible*, pages 1371–1387; available online at esv.org.)

1. Israel Has Been a Faithless Spouse (2:1–3:5)

The Lord begins by recalling his love for the people of Israel. What are some of the ways he showed his covenant love for them? (Look especially at 2:1–7.)

Despite Yahweh's extravagant love, Israel has "changed its gods, even though they are no gods[?] . . . my people have changed their glory for that which does not profit" (2:11). What does it mean that they have "hewed out cisterns for themselves, broken cisterns that can hold no water" (v. 13)?

2. Israel Can and Should Repent (3:6–4:4)

Despite seeing God judge the northern kingdom of Israel for its idolatry, Judah not only followed in her footsteps but surpassed her in wickedness (3:6–11). So Yahweh calls Judah to "return," or repent. According to 3:12–14, what does repentance look like? (You may want also to consult 3:19–25 and 4:1–4.)

According to 3:15–18, what does God promise to do for those who repent?

3. Disaster Is Coming (4:5–31)

God now instructs Jeremiah to warn Judah of the coming judgment. The disaster is coming "from the north" (4:6) in the form of the Babylonians. What images of judgment are used in this section (vv. 7–18)?

What does Jeremiah's use of language from Genesis 1 tell us about the coming judgment (4:23–26)?

4. Judah's Unwillingness to Repent and Its Consequences (5:1–31)

Despite warnings of judgment (4:5–31) and promises of restoration (3:15–18), Judah is not interested in repentance. Look at 5:1–13. What classes of people have sinned and angered Yahweh? What reasons does God give for not pardoning Judah?

5. God Has Rejected His People (6:1–30)

Yahweh's judgment will sweep across the whole land, from the least to the greatest (6:1–15). According to 6:16, how should the people respond to the warnings of judgment?

Compare Yahweh's words in 6:16 with Psalm 1 and Jesus' words in Matthew 11:28–30. In light of these comparisons, what does it mean for believers to walk in the "ancient paths"?

Read through the following three sections on *Gospel Glimpses, Whole-Bible Connections*, and *Theological Soundings*. Then take time to consider the *Personal Implications* these sections may have for you.

Gospel Glimpses

REPENTANCE. Central to Jeremiah's message is the call to repent (Jer. 3:6–14, 19–25), to turn away from sin (4:1–4). The very first words of Jesus' preaching ministry strike a similar note: "The time is fulfilled, and the kingdom of God is at hand; repent and believe in the gospel" (Mark 1:15). When the crowds at Pentecost ask Peter how they should respond to his gospel message, he tells them, "Repent and be baptized every one of you in the name of Jesus Christ for the forgiveness of your sins, and you will receive the gift of the Holy Spirit" (Acts 2:38). Repentance is God's gracious gift to his people (2 Tim. 2:25).

THE ANCIENT PATHS. Instead of pursuing false gods, God's people are called to pursue the ancient paths (Jer. 6:16). In a world constantly looking for the next big thing, God calls us to walk in the way of the righteous (Ps. 1:1–6). Just as God promised rest for the souls of those who walk in the ancient paths, Jesus promised, "Come to me, all who labor and are heavy laden, and I will give you rest" (Matt. 11:28). Through the gospel God gives us rest from our sins and from the burden of trying to earn his favor.

Whole-Bible Connections

SHEPHERDS. Jeremiah foresees a day when God would raise up shepherds after his own heart (Jer. 3:15–18). This not only harkens back to David (1 Sam. 13:14) and echoes what Ezekiel promised (Ezek. 34:20–24); it also points forward to David's greater son, Jesus Christ (Acts 13:22–23). He is the Good Shepherd who lays down his life for the sheep (John 10:11–15). God has also given his church undershepherds (elders) to feed his people the life-giving nourishment of his Word (Acts 6:1–7; 1 Pet. 5:1–5).

WE RESEMBLE WHAT WE WORSHIP. When Judah went after worthless idols, they themselves became worthless (Jer. 2:5). God created us to resemble what we worship; when we worship idols that are blind, deaf, and dumb, we begin to take on those characteristics. But through the gospel, Jesus turns us into people who worship God "in spirit and truth"(John 4:24). As we see Christ in all his beauty, we are changed to reflect his glory (2 Cor. 3:18; 1 John 3:1–3).

▶ Theological Soundings

HUMAN SINFULNESS. While the specifics of how sin manifests itself may vary from person to person and from culture to culture, the reality of sin remains the same. As Romans 3:23 puts it, "All have sinned and fall short of the glory of God." Sin entered the world through Adam and has spread to all humanity (Rom. 5:12–14). Sin affects the entirety of our being, and hence is sometimes referred to as "total depravity."[2]

GOD'S PATIENCE. Time after time God sent his prophets to Judah, displaying his patience. When God revealed himself to Moses, he described himself as "the LORD, the LORD, a God merciful and gracious, slow to anger, and abounding in steadfast love and faithfulness" (Ex. 34:6). This patience should not be mistaken for indifference, however; we must not "presume on the riches of his kindness and forbearance and patience, not knowing that God's kindness is meant to lead [us] to repentance" (Rom. 2:4).

▶ Personal Implications

Take time to reflect on the implications of Jeremiah 2:1–6:30 for your own life today. Consider what you have learned that might lead you to praise God, repent of sin, and trust in his gracious promises. Make notes below on the personal implications for your walk with the Lord of the (1) *Gospel Glimpses*, (2) *Whole-Bible Connections*, (3) *Theological Soundings*, and (4) this passage as a whole.

1. Gospel Glimpses

2. Whole-Bible Connections

3. Theological Soundings

4. Jeremiah 2:1–6:30

As You Finish This Unit . . .

Take a moment now to ask for the Lord's blessing and help as you continue in this study of Jeremiah. And take a moment also to look back through this unit of study, to reflect on key things that the Lord may be teaching you—and perhaps to highlight and underline these things to review again in the future.

Definitions

[1] **Yahweh** – The likely English form of the name represented by the Hebrew letters *YHWH*. The Lord revealed this unique name for himself (meaning "I am") to Moses at the burning bush, telling him to instruct the Israelites to call on him by this name (Ex. 3:14–15). English translations of the Bible usually render this term as "Lord," with small capital letters. (*YHWH* can also be translated God, with small capitals.)

[2] **Depravity** – The sinful condition of human nature apart from grace, whereby humans are inclined to serve their own will and desires and to reject God's rule.

Week 4: False Religion and an Idolatrous People

Jeremiah 7:1–10:25

The Place of the Passage

In Jeremiah 7:1–10:25, the prophet provides further support for God's charges against Judah. They hypocritically take comfort in the temple while living in open disobedience to God (7:1–8:3); they reject Yahweh's Torah[1] (8:4–17), grieve Jeremiah with their deceitful lives (8:18–9:26), and continue to practice idolatry (10:1–16). As a result, exile awaits (10:17–25).

The Big Picture

In this section of Jeremiah, we see that Yahweh wants his people to know him for who he truly is and live a life of covenant faithfulness as a result.

Reflection and Discussion

Read through the complete passage for this study, Jeremiah 7:1–10:25. Then review the questions below and write out your answers. (For further background, see the *ESV Study Bible*, pages 1387–1395; available online at esv.org.)

1. Judah's Improper Reliance on the Temple (7:1–8:3)

What were the people putting their confidence in to avoid destruction by the Babylonians? Why was this confidence so misplaced?

How were the people living as a result of their misplaced confidence?

God commands Jeremiah not to pray for the people (7:16). What reasons does he give (vv. 17–18)? Why is this situation different from Moses interceding for the Israelites when they sinned with the golden calf (Exodus 32–34)?

2. Judah Rejects God's Torah (8:4–17)

Because they reject the Law of the Lord, the people are continually backsliding; they are worse than animals, who at least know the seasons (8:4–7). What role have Judah's leaders played in the failures of the people (vv. 8–15)?

3. Jeremiah Grieves Judah's Deceitful Living (8:18–9:26)

How does Jeremiah's grief express itself? How does it compare to Paul's grief in Romans 9:1–5?

Jeremiah gives several examples of Judah's deceitful living (9:3–9). Which of these examples stands out to you? Do any in particular hit close to home for you?

Twice in this passage (vv. 12–16 and vv. 23–24) Yahweh refers to the need for wisdom. What do we learn about wisdom from these passages?

Read 1 Corinthians 1:18–31. How does Paul apply Jeremiah 9:24 to believers?

Since God wants us to know him for who he truly is, what attributes[2] of Yahweh are emphasized in 9:23–26? How does this list compare with what God reveals about himself in Exodus 34:6–7?

4. Judah Engages in Idolatry and Will Be Sent into Exile (10:1–25)

In the opening section of this passage (10:1–16), a contrast is drawn between idols and Yahweh, the true and living god. How is Yahweh distinguished from the idols of the nations?

Once again Yahweh promises to send Judah into exile for their sin (10:17–22). How does Jeremiah respond (vv. 23–24)? Why do you think he responds in this way?

Read through the following three sections on *Gospel Glimpses, Whole-Bible Connections*, and *Theological Soundings*. Then take time to consider the *Personal Implications* these sections may have for you.

Gospel Glimpses

GOD DELIGHTS IN BEING KNOWN FOR WHO HE TRULY IS. God delights in his people knowing him, and he wants to ensure that we know him as he truly is (Jer. 9:24). He wants us to know him as "the LORD, the LORD, a God merciful and gracious, slow to anger, and abounding in steadfast love and faithfulness" (Ex. 34:6–7). Despite our rebellion against him, God took on flesh and dwelled among us in the person of Jesus Christ, who was "full of grace and truth" (John 1:14). Because of what he has done for us by his dying and rising, we can experience the "surpassing worth of knowing Christ Jesus [our] Lord" and the "power of his resurrection" (Phil. 3:8, 10).

GOD GIVES HIS PEOPLE PROPHETS. God repeatedly sent prophets to turn his people back to him (Jer. 7:25). He uses those same prophets today through their written words in Scripture (Rom. 15:4). But in the person of Jesus Christ we have the prophet greater than Moses (Deut. 18:18; Acts 3:22–23), who not only spoke God's word but obeyed it perfectly for us (Phil. 2:8).

Whole-Bible Connections

TEMPLE. God created the garden of Eden as his sanctuary to dwell with his people (Gen. 2:4–17). After he brought Israel out of Egypt, he instructed them to build the tabernacle for him to live among his people (Ex. 25:1–9). King Solomon built the temple as a more permanent place for God to dwell with his people in the Promised Land (1 Kings 7–8). These structures pointed forward to the true temple, Jesus Christ (John 1:14; 2:21). All who are united to him by faith are being built into a temple for God's Spirit to indwell (Eph. 2:19–22; 1 Pet. 2:4–8).

"I WILL BE YOUR GOD, AND YOU SHALL BE MY PEOPLE." God's purpose in making a covenant with Israel was to be their God and for them to be his people (Lev. 26:12), but Israel broke that covenant through idolatry and rebellion (Jer. 7:23–26). Because of what Jesus has done for us, God says to believers, "I will be [your] God, and [you] shall be my people" (2 Cor. 6:16). So we await eagerly the new heaven and earth, where God will dwell with his people in all his fullness and we will be his glorified people (Rev. 21:3).

Theological Soundings

HYPOCRISY AND THE HUMAN HEART. The human heart is so deceitful that we can go through outward motions of worship while living in obvious sin (Isa. 1:10–20; Jer. 7:1–26; Mark 7:1–13). But true worship involves both proper heart orientation and outward expression of devotion to the Lord. We may fool others by our outward behavior, but we never fool God, who sees the heart (1 Sam. 16:7).

GOD'S CHARACTER. God reveals himself as one who is full of mercy and grace, yet who will execute justice to punish the guilty (Ex. 34:6–7; Jer. 9:24). But how can God extend mercy to the guilty without compromising his justice? The answer is the cross: Jesus is our sinless substitute who experienced the punishment we deserve for our sins, so we receive God's mercy through being united to Christ by faith (Rom. 3:25–26).

Personal Implications

Take time to reflect on the implications of Jeremiah 7:1–10:25 for your own life today. Consider what you have learned that might lead you to praise God, repent of sin, and trust in his gracious promises. Make notes below on the personal implications for your walk with the Lord of the (1) *Gospel Glimpses*, (2) *Whole-Bible Connections*, (3) *Theological Soundings*, and (4) this passage as a whole.

1. Gospel Glimpses

2. Whole-Bible Connections

3. Theological Soundings

_____

_____

_____

_____

_____

_____

4. Jeremiah 7:1–10:25

_____

_____

_____

_____

_____

_____

_____

> ## As You Finish This Unit . . .

Take a moment now to ask for the Lord's blessing and help as you continue in this study of Jeremiah. And take a moment also to look back through this unit of study, to reflect on some key things that the Lord may be teaching you—and perhaps to highlight and underline these things to review again in the future.

Definitions

[1] **Torah** – The first five books of the Bible, also called the Law or the Pentateuch.

[2] **Attributes of God** – The distinctive characteristics of God as he is described in the Bible. These include eternality, faithfulness, goodness, graciousness, holiness, immutability, infinitude, justice, love, mercy, omnipotence, omnipresence, omniscience, self-existence, self-sufficiency, sovereignty, and wisdom.

WEEK 5: JEREMIAH'S STRUGGLES WITH GOD AND JUDAH

Jeremiah 11:1–20:18

▲

The Place of the Passage

After two sections focusing on Israel's covenant adultery (Jer. 2:1–6:30) and idolatrous false worship (7:1–10:25), Jeremiah 11:1–20:18 narrates the prophet's struggles with both God and Judah. Because of the opposition he must endure (11:1–12:17), Jeremiah feels betrayed by God (13:1–15:21). Despite the Lord's renewing Jeremiah (16:1–17:18), the prophet continues to feel the weight of constant opposition (17:19–18:23). Nevertheless, Jeremiah perseveres amid his suffering, despite questioning his calling (19:1–20:18).

The Big Picture

Jeremiah 11:1–20:18 vividly portrays the struggle to remain faithful to God's call amid repeated opposition.

> ## Reflection and Discussion

Read through the complete passage for this study, Jeremiah 11:1–20:18. Then review the questions below concerning this section of Jeremiah and write your notes on them. (For further background, see the *ESV Study Bible*, pages 1395–1411; available online at esv.org.)

1. Jeremiah Surprised by Opposition (11:1–12:17)

In 11:1–17 Jeremiah highlights Israel's repeated covenant breaking. What covenant promises does he mention in verses 1–13? Why did Israel repeatedly fail?

Because of Israel's unfaithfulness, God instructs Jeremiah not to pray for them. How does Jeremiah respond to this unusual command (11:18–12:4)? What is God's response (12:5–13)?

2. Jeremiah Feels Betrayed by God (13:1–15:21)

Jeremiah uses two parables[1] to portray Judah as a ruined (13:1–11) and drunken (vv. 12–14) nation. As a result Yahweh will send them into exile (vv. 15–27). The people fail to realize that the drought in the land is a foretaste of coming judgment (14:1–6). This prompts Jeremiah to pray for the people; in what does he ground his prayers (14:7–10, 19–22)?

Yahweh reiterates his command not to pray for the people because of their sin, and condemns the false prophets who are claiming to speak for Yahweh by promising peace (14:13–18). The Lord says that Judah's condition is so bad that he would not even listen to Moses and Samuel if they were to intercede; instead God will send "four kinds of destroyers" (15:1–9). Jeremiah then complains about the difficulties he is facing (15:10–14). What is Jeremiah's complaint, and how does Yahweh respond (15:15–21)?

----

3. Jeremiah Renewed by God (16:1–17:18)

Jeremiah responds positively to God's rebuke and continues his ministry. He preaches about the terrible times awaiting Judah (16:1–13), but then announces that judgment will not be the final word (vv. 14–21). What will this promised restoration look like? What light does Matthew 4:18–22 shed on the promise to send "many fishers" (Jer. 16:16)?

Jeremiah 17:1–13 draws a sharp contrast between those who trust in humanity and those who trust in the Lord. Fill in the chart below for both sides of the contrast:

Those who trust in humanity	Those who trust in the Lord

What does this passage (17:1–13) tell us about the human heart? How does this compare to what Jesus says about the heart in Mark 7:14–23?

----

4. Jeremiah Burdened by Opposition (17:19–18:23)

Jeremiah remains faithful to his calling, but Judah remains "faithful" in its opposition to him! After condemning Judah's repeated breaking of the Sabbath (17:19–27), Yahweh sends Jeremiah to the potter's house for an object lesson (18:1–17). What is the main point of this object lesson, and how is it applied? How does Paul use similar imagery in Romans 9:14–24?

----

5. Jeremiah Endures Suffering and Questions His Calling (19:1–20:18)

After yet another visual parable (breaking a flask) symbolizing the destruction of Judah (19:1–13), Pashhur the priest beats Jeremiah and puts him in stocks (20:1–2). In response, Jeremiah reiterates Yahweh's impending judgment on

Judah, singling out Pashhur's death in exile in Babylon (vv. 3–6). How would you characterize Jeremiah's response to these events (vv. 7–18)? What aspects of God's character does Jeremiah mention?

Read through the following three sections on *Gospel Glimpses*, *Whole-Bible Connections*, and *Theological Soundings*. Then take time to consider the *Personal Implications* these sections may have for you.

Gospel Glimpses

CREATED TO DISPLAY GOD'S GLORY. God intended Judah to "be for me a people, a name, a praise, and a glory, but they would not listen" (Jer. 13:11). Because of their sin, they failed to reflect God's glory. But the good news of the gospel is that "God, who said, 'Let light shine out of darkness,' has shone in our hearts to give the light of the knowledge of the glory of God in the face of Jesus Christ" (2 Cor. 4:6). As we see the glory of Christ, we "are being transformed into the same image from one degree of glory to another" (2 Cor. 3:18).

HEART TRANSFORMATION. Because of sin entering the world, the human heart "is deceitful above all things, and desperately sick" (Jer. 17:9). Jesus affirmed this reality when he said, "From within, out of the heart of man, come evil thoughts, sexual immorality, theft, murder, adultery, coveting, wickedness, deceit, sensuality, envy, slander, pride, foolishness. All these evil things come from within, and they defile a person" (Mark 7:21–23). But when the Spirit causes us to be born again, God gives us a new heart (Ezek. 36:26; 2 Cor. 3:3). God writes his law on our hearts and causes us to walk in his ways so that we "become obedient from the heart" (Jer. 31:33; Ezek. 36:27; Rom. 6:17).

Whole-Bible Connections

NEW EXODUS/RETURN FROM EXILE. The exodus from Egypt was the defining act of redemption for Israel. But God promises that Israel's return from exile would be even greater (Jer. 16:14–15). Although a remnant of the people returned to the land after 70 years of exile (Ezra 1:1–11), it was evident that not all the promises of restoration had come to pass. Through the work of Jesus Christ, God has begun regathering his people (Matt. 4:12–25; Rom. 9:19–33). As the gospel is preached, Jew and Gentile alike are being gathered into a remnant seeking the Lord (Acts 15:12–20).

FISHERS TO GATHER GOD'S PEOPLE. As part of God's plan to bring his people back from exile, he promises, "I am sending for many fishers" to catch them (Jer. 16:16). To signal that the promised return from exile had finally begun through his life and ministry, Jesus called Peter and his brother Andrew to "Follow me, and I will make you fishers of men" (Matt. 4:19). After his resurrection Jesus sends out all his people to continue this work when he says, "Go therefore and make disciples of all nations, baptizing them in the name of the Father and of the Son and of the Holy Spirit, teaching them to observe all that I have commanded you" (Matt. 28:19–20).

Theological Soundings

PRAYER BASED ON GOD'S CHARACTER. Following in the footsteps of Moses (Ex. 33:12–16), Jeremiah prays for God to act on behalf of his people "for your name's sake" (Jer. 14:9, 21). Daniel begins his lengthy prayer by saying, "O Lord, the great and awesome God, who keeps covenant and steadfast love with those who love him and keep his commandments" (Dan. 9:4). Nehemiah begins his prayer of confession by acknowledging God as the Creator and covenant-making God (Neh. 9:6–8). Since we have nothing in ourselves on which to base our prayers, we must approach the Lord on the basis of his character and commitment to display his glory.

GOD'S SOVEREIGNTY. The parable of the potter and his vessel emphasizes God's sovereignty,[2] his right to do as he pleases (Jer. 18:1–11). Paul alludes to this passage when he asserts God's sovereignty to elect some to salvation and to pass over others (Rom. 9:14–23). In our human arrogance we naturally chafe against this, but as the Creator, Yahweh "is in the heavens; he does all that he pleases" (Ps. 115:3).

Personal Implications

Take time to reflect on the implications of Jeremiah 11:1–20:18 for your own life today. Consider what you have learned that might lead you to praise God, repent of sin, and trust in his gracious promises. Make notes below on the personal implications for your walk with the Lord of the (1) *Gospel Glimpses*, (2) *Whole-Bible Connections*, (3) *Theological Soundings*, and (4) this passage as a whole.

1. Gospel Glimpses

2. Whole-Bible Connections

3. Theological Soundings

4. Jeremiah 11:1–20:18

> ## As You Finish This Unit . . .

Take a moment now to ask for the Lord's blessing and help as you continue in this study of Jeremiah. And take a moment also to look back through this unit of study, to reflect on some key things that the Lord may be teaching you—and perhaps to highlight and underline these things to review again in the future.

Definitions

[1] **Parable** – A story that uses everyday imagery and activities to communicate a spiritual truth. Jesus often taught in parables (e.g., Matthew 13).

[2] **Sovereignty** – Supreme and independent power and authority. Sovereignty over all things is a distinctive attribute of God (1 Tim. 6:15–16). He directs all things to carry out his purposes (Rom. 8:28–29).

WEEK 6: JEREMIAH'S CONFRONTATIONS

Jeremiah 21:1–29:32

▲

The Place of the Passage

Because Yahweh is with Jeremiah "as a dread warrior" (Jer. 20:11), he is able to confront and confound his opponents and their beliefs. God had promised Jeremiah that opponents "will fight against you, but they shall not prevail against you, for I am with you, declares the LORD, to deliver you" (1:19). So it comes as no surprise that Jeremiah goes toe to toe with kings (21:1–23:8), false prophets (23:9–40), the people (24:1–25:38), and false belief (26:1–29:32). Yet through it all, and through all the pressures under which it puts him, Jeremiah remains faithful to proclaim God's word.

The Big Picture

Jeremiah 21:1–29:32 shows us that God keeps his covenant promises by confronting sin and promising restoration to those who trust in the righteous Branch.

> ## Reflection and Discussion

Read through Jeremiah 21:1–29:32, which will be the focus of this week's study. Following this, review the questions below concerning this section of the book of Jeremiah and write your responses. (For further background, see the *ESV Study Bible*, pages 1411–1425; available online at esv.org.)

1. Jeremiah Opposes Judah's Kings (21:1–23:8)

Zedekiah, the last king of Judah (597–586 BC), asks Jeremiah to inquire of Yahweh (perhaps in 588 BC, when he refused to pay tribute to Babylon; 21:1–2). Yahweh warns that he himself will fight against Judah, and those who survive will be taken into exile (21:3–7). Those who stay in the city will die, while those who surrender to the Chaldeans will live (21:8–10). In contrast to King Zedekiah's behavior, how were the kings of God's people supposed to behave (21:11–22:10)?

The leaders of God's people are frequently called shepherds. According to Jeremiah 23:1–2, what were the shepherds in his day doing? Look at Ezekiel 34:1–10 to see what God says about these same shepherds. In John 10:1–18 Jesus describes himself as the Good Shepherd; what does Jesus do, and do differently, that makes him the Good Shepherd?

Yahweh promises to "raise up for David a righteous Branch" to rule over and save God's people; he will be called "The Lord is our righteousness"[1] (23:5–8).

According to 1 Corinthians 1:30, how is this passage fulfilled? Based on Romans 5:12–21, how did that fulfillment take place?

2. Jeremiah Opposes False Prophets (23:9–40)

Prophets were supposed to preach God's covenant and make accurate predictions (Deut. 13:1–11; 18:15–22). But Jeremiah was forced to contend with false prophets. What does he observe about these false prophets (Jer. 23:9–15)? What is God's perspective on them (23:16–32)?

3. Jeremiah Opposes the People (24:1–25:38)

In 597 BC King Nebuchadnezzar of Babylon took a second wave of exiles to Babylon, including many of the elite from Judah (King Jeconiah and the prophet Ezekiel among them), and installed Zedekiah as king of Judah. Soon after, God shows Jeremiah a vision of two baskets of figs (Jer. 24:1–10). The basket of bad figs represents the officials of Judah remaining in the land, who will experience God's judgment. The basket of good figs represents those exiled to Babylon, whom God will one day bring back to the land of Israel. What does God promise to those he will bring back to the land? Where have we seen the language of verse 6 earlier in Jeremiah?

In Jeremiah 24:7 God promises, "I will give them a heart to know that I am the Lord." What does it mean for God to give someone a new heart? Consult Deuteronomy 30:6 and Ezekiel 36:26–28 to fill out your answer.

In Jeremiah 25 the scene shifts back to 605 BC, when Nebuchadnezzar took his first wave of exiles to Babylon (including Daniel, Shadrach, Meshach, and Abednego; see Dan. 1:1–5). Jeremiah has been preaching his message of repentance and impending judgment, yet Judah has failed to listen (Jer. 25:1–7). According to 25:8–14, what will God do to Babylon? When will this take place? What reason does 2 Chronicles 36:20–21 give for the specific amount of time designated by Jeremiah?

The message of God's impending judgment continues in Jeremiah 25:15–27. What symbol does God use to portray this judgment? What light does this passage shed on Jesus' agony in Gethsemane (Matt. 26:36–46)? What was Jesus contemplating as he prayed there?

4. Jeremiah Opposes False Belief (26:1–29:32)

Jeremiah 26 flashes *back* to 609 BC, after the death of King Josiah and the three-month reign of his son Jehoahaz. The new king is Jehoiakim (609–598), another son of Josiah. Yahweh instructs Jeremiah to stand in the court of the temple and announce Yahweh's impending judgment if Judah does not repent (Jer. 26:1–6). The leaders threaten to kill Jeremiah (vv. 7–11) but eventually change their mind (vv. 12–24).

Jeremiah 27 flashes *forward* to the beginning of the reign of Zedekiah in 597 BC. Yahweh commands Jeremiah to illustrate submission to Nebuchadnezzar with yoke bars, warning that Judah will not escape his rule and exile. Several years *later* (594/593 BC) the false prophet Hananiah responds (ch. 28), claiming that Yahweh will break the yoke of Babylon, return the temple vessels, and bring back the exiles. He symbolizes this by breaking Jeremiah's yoke bars. Soon afterward, Yahweh reassures Jeremiah that Hananiah's words are not from him, promising that Hananiah will die within the year—which happens just as Yahweh has foretold.

In chapter 29, the scene shifts *back* to 597, when Babylon took the second wave of exiles (including the prophet Ezekiel). Some (e.g., Daniel and his friends) had already been in Babylon for eight years, while others had been there for just a few months. God inspires Jeremiah to write a letter instructing the exiles on how to conduct themselves in Babylon. What instructions does God give the exiles (29:1–9)?

What does Yahweh promise to do for the exiles (29:10–14)?

Read through the following three sections on *Gospel Glimpses*, *Whole-Bible Connections*, and *Theological Soundings*. Then take time to consider the *Personal Implications* these sections may have for you.

Gospel Glimpses

SEEKING THE LORD WHOLEHEARTEDLY. Twice in this section Yahweh speaks of a day when his people will seek him with their whole heart (Jer. 24:6–7; 29:12–14). Both Moses (Deut. 30:6) and Ezekiel (Ezek. 36:26–27) looked forward to a day when God would "circumcise" people's hearts to seek him. That happens when the Holy Spirit causes a person to be born again (John 3:3–8; Rom. 2:29) and we are changed so that we seek God's kingdom first (Matt. 6:33). Jesus invites us to "Ask, and it will be given to you; seek, and you will find; knock, and it will be opened to you. For everyone who asks receives, and the one who seeks finds, and to the one who knocks it will be opened" (Matt. 7:7–8).

GOD WORKS FOR THE GOOD OF HIS PEOPLE. Amid the exile, God swears that his plans for his people are for their good (Jer. 24:6–7; 29:10–14). This did not mean a life of prosperity and ease, but that everything God was doing was for their ultimate good. God makes the same promise to us in Romans 8:28, grounding it in what God has done for us in Christ: "Those whom he foreknew he also predestined to be conformed to the image of his Son, in order that he might be the firstborn among many brothers. And those whom he predestined he also called, and those whom he called he also justified, and those whom he justified he also glorified" (Rom. 8:29–30).

Whole-Bible Connections

A RIGHTEOUS BRANCH. God had promised David that he would raise up one of his descendants to rule over an eternal kingdom (2 Sam. 7:12–16). Yahweh reaffirms that promise when he swears to "raise up for David a righteous Branch" who will rule wisely and justly (Jer. 23:5). His name will be "The LORD is our righteousness" (Jer. 23:6), a promise fulfilled in Jesus Christ, who as a descendant of David (Rom. 1:3) "became to us wisdom from God, righteousness and sanctification and redemption" (1 Cor. 1:30). God "made him to be sin who knew no sin, so that in him we might become the righteousness of God" (2 Cor. 5:21).

THE CUP OF GOD'S WRATH.[2] God's righteous wrath toward human rebellion is often portrayed as a cup that will be poured out or drunk (Ps. 75:8; Isa. 51:17–23; Jer. 25:15–27). This is the cup that Jesus contemplates the night before his crucifixion when he prays three times, "My Father, if it be possible, let this cup pass from me; nevertheless, not as I will, but as you will" (Matt. 26:39, 42, 44). On the cross Jesus drank the cup of God's wrath stored up for his people so that they would not have to drink it themselves (Matt. 27:45–50; Rom. 3:21–26). As a result, "There is therefore now no condemnation for those who are in Christ Jesus" (Rom. 8:1). There will come a day when God will pour out his cup of wrath on all the wicked (Rev. 14:10; 16:19; 17:4; 18:6) who have not turned to Christ.

Theological Soundings

TRUE VERSUS FALSE PROPHECY. Throughout his lifetime Jeremiah had to deal with false prophets claiming to speak in the name of the Lord (e.g., Jer. 23:9–40; 28:1–17; 29:15–32). Moses warned that a prophet's words must be tested by their fidelity to what the Lord has already revealed and by whether what they prophesy comes to pass (Deut. 18:21–22). As believers, we have the words of true prophets confirmed in Scripture itself (1 Pet. 1:10–12).

THE WORD OF THE LORD. In contrast to the empty words of false prophets, God's words are like a fire and a hammer that smashes rock (Jer. 23:29). Yahweh says that his word "shall not return to me empty, but it shall accomplish that which I purpose, and shall succeed in the thing for which I sent it" (Isa. 55:11). Elsewhere the word of the Lord is described as "sharper than any two-edged sword, piercing to the division of soul and of spirit, of joints and of marrow, and discerning the thoughts and intentions of the heart" (Heb. 4:12). What a privilege it is for us to have this word of the Lord in written form to read, study, memorize, and apply!

Personal Implications

Take time to reflect on the implications of Jeremiah 21:1–29:32 for your own life today. Consider what you have learned that might lead you to praise God, repent of sin, and trust in his gracious promises. Make notes below on the personal implications for your walk with the Lord of the (1) *Gospel Glimpses*, (2) *Whole-Bible Connections*, (3) *Theological Soundings*, and (4) this passage as a whole.

1. Gospel Glimpses

2. Whole-Bible Connections

3. Theological Soundings

4. Jeremiah 21:1–29:32

As You Finish This Unit . . .

Take a moment now to ask for the Lord's blessing and help as you continue in this study of Jeremiah. And take a moment also to look back through this unit of study, to reflect on some key things that the Lord may be teaching you—and perhaps to highlight and underline these things to review again in the future.

Definitions

[1] **Righteousness** – The state of being morally right and without sin. One of God's distinctive attributes. God imputes righteousness to (justifies) sinners who trust in Jesus Christ.

[2] **Wrath** – God's righteous anger toward sin, as an expression of his holiness.

Week 7: Restoration for Judah and Israel

Jeremiah 30:1–33:26

The Place of the Passage

Restoration and redemption—minor chords in Jeremiah's symphony to this point—come to the forefront in chapters 30–33. Sometimes referred to as the Book of Comfort, this section of Jeremiah makes clear that judgment will not be the final word. God will restore the nation (Jer. 30:1–24), make a new covenant with Israel (31:1–40), bring Israel back to the Promised Land (32:1–44), and fulfill the promises of his covenant with David (33:1–26).

The Big Picture

In Jeremiah 30–33 God comforts his people by promising to deal with their sin once for all and to renew creation through a Davidic king who will institute a new covenant.

> ### Reflection and Discussion

Read through the complete passage for this study, Jeremiah 30:1–33:26. Then review the questions below concerning this central section of the book and write your notes on them. (For further background, see the *ESV Study Bible*, pages 1426–1436; available online at esv.org.)

1. God Will Restore the Nation (30:1–24)

This chapter serves as an introduction to the entire section (Jer. 30:1–33:26). In the opening passage (30:1–11), what does God promise to do for his people?

Yahweh promises his people that "all who devour you shall be devoured . . . those who plunder you shall be plundered, and all who prey on you I will make a prey" (Jer. 30:16); "I will multiply them, and they shall not be few; I will make them honored, and they shall not be small" (v. 19). Compare this with the language of his promise to Abraham in Genesis 12:1–3. What do these similarities tell us about what God promises to do here in Jeremiah 30?

2. God Will Make a New Covenant with Israel (31:1–40)

Yahweh promises to restore his people (Jer. 31:1–6) and calls them to rejoice at the news (vv. 7–9). He warns the nations of what he is about to do for his people (vv. 10–14). Exiled Judah is personified as Rachel (Jacob's favorite wife; Gen. 29:30) weeping at the exile of God's people (Jer. 31:15), but Yahweh reassures her that the promise of comfort is real and the people will return to the land (vv. 16–26). God will "sow" his people in the land, "build" them, and "plant" them there (vv. 27–28). What does the proverb in verse 29 mean? What is its significance?

Jeremiah 31:31–34 describes the new covenant God promises to make with his people. What are the various elements of this new covenant?

In what ways will the new covenant be different from the old one?

Celebrating Passover[1] on the night before his crucifixion, Jesus said, "This cup that is poured out for you is the new covenant in my blood" (Luke 22:20). What light does Luke 22:14–23 shed on the new covenant promised in Jeremiah 31:34? What additional insight does 2 Corinthians 3:1–18 add to our understanding of this new covenant?

3. God Will Bring Israel Back to the Promised Land (32:1–44)

By 588–587 BC, Nebuchadnezzar had laid siege to Jerusalem (32:1–2). While Jeremiah is under arrest by order of King Zedekiah, God commands the prophet to buy a field as a sign that "houses and fields and vineyards shall again be bought in this land" (vv. 2–15). What is Jeremiah's response to God's command (vv. 16–25)?

Yahweh assures Jeremiah that nothing is too difficult for him (32:26–35). Although the expression "new covenant" is not used, it is described in verses 36–44. What else do we learn in these verses about this new covenant, beyond what we learned in 31:31–34?

God promises to "give them one heart and one way, that they may fear me forever, for their own good and the good of their children after them" (32:39). What does this mean in light of passages like Deuteronomy 6:4–9, Psalm 86:8–13, Ezekiel 11:19–20, and Matthew 22:34–40?

4. God Will Honor the Davidic Covenant (33:1–26)

Although judgment will indeed come (Jer. 33:1–5), restoration is also certain (vv. 6–13). This restoration will be in fulfillment of God's covenant promises to David (vv. 14–26). In 2 Samuel 7:12–16 God had promised that David's descendant would rule over an eternal kingdom. In Jeremiah 23:5–6 this descendant of David is called a "righteous Branch," whose name will be "The LORD is our righteousness." Here in 33:15–16, the righteous Branch is mentioned, but this time it is the redeemed people of God who are called "The LORD is our righteousness." What does this tell us about the relationship between the promised king and his redeemed people? (Hint: see 2 Cor. 5:21.)

What does it mean that David and the priests will never lack a man to fill their roles (Jer. 33:17–26)? Look at Romans 1:1–5; 12:1–2; and 1 Peter 2:9–10 for help if necessary.

Read through the following three sections on *Gospel Glimpses*, *Whole-Bible Connections*, and *Theological Soundings*. Then take time to consider the *Personal Implications* these sections may have for you.

Gospel Glimpses

FORGIVENESS OF SIN. In announcing the new covenant, God promises, "I will forgive their iniquity, and I will remember their sin no more" (Jer. 31:34). Although God appointed the sacrificial system to deal with Israel's sin, "it is impossible for the blood of bulls and goats to take away sins" (Heb. 10:4). These sacrifices pointed forward to the one who would offer himself as a sacrifice for sin (Isa. 53:10; Gal. 1:4). Through his death on the cross, Jesus paid the price for the sins of his people once and for all (Heb. 9:24–28). All who turn from their sin and trust in Jesus Christ experience God's forgiveness (Acts 2:38).

GOD'S LAW WRITTEN ON OUR HEARTS. Not only does the new covenant hold the promise of forgiveness of sins; God also promises to write his law on the hearts of his people (Jer. 31:33). That is exactly what God has done through his Spirit for those who believe in Christ (Rom. 2:29; 2 Cor. 3:1–3). By his Spirit dwelling inside us, God is the one "who works in you, both to will and to work for his good pleasure" (Phil. 2:13). The Holy Spirit produces his fruit in our lives: "love, joy, peace, patience, kindness, goodness, faithfulness, gentleness, self-control," and "against such things there is no law" (Gal. 5:22–23).

Whole-Bible Connections

GOD'S COVENANT WITH DAVID. Despite Israel and Judah's persistent disobedience, God remains committed to fulfill his promise to David (Jer. 33:14–26). Thus when Matthew introduces the genealogy of Jesus, he identifies him as "the son of David, the son of Abraham" (Matt. 1:1). People in need repeatedly call Jesus "Son of David" when asking him to heal them (Matt. 9:27; 15:22; 20:30–31). Peter makes clear that the promises made to David find their fulfillment in Jesus Christ (Acts 2:22–36). As the "Root of David," Jesus Christ is the one who, in the words and imagery of Revelation, "has conquered, so that he can open the scroll and its seven seals" (Rev. 5:5; 22:16).

RACHEL WEEPING FOR HER CHILDREN. Judah is so despondent at her devastation that she cannot even believe the promises of restoration (Jer. 31:15). Yahweh reassures her that despite her grief he will forgive and restore her (vv. 16–40). Matthew picks up this language to describe the grief of those in Bethlehem when Herod massacred their children in his efforts to kill the Christ child (Matt. 2:16–18). Yet, amid such tragic grief, God was working out his purposes to end his people's spiritual exile, and that of Gentiles too, through Jesus Christ.

Theological Soundings

IMPUTATION.[2] God promises to raise up a righteous Branch as a king to rule over his people; that king will be called "The LORD is our righteousness" (Jer. 23:5–6). That promise is repeated in 33:14–16, but this time the name "The LORD is our righteousness" is given to the redeemed city of Jerusalem. The righteous Branch gives his righteousness to his redeemed people. In the same way, Jesus Christ gives his own righteousness to his people, that is, to believers. This is simply another way of saying that "for our sake he [God] made him [Christ] to be sin who knew no sin, so that in him we might become the righteousness of God" (2 Cor. 5:21).

YAHWEH AS CREATOR. The Bible makes clear that Yahweh is the Creator and sustainer of everything (Genesis 1–2). The Lord reminds his people of this fact to engender confidence that he will fulfill his promises (Jer. 31:35–37; 33:20–26). Isaiah 54:10 captures this reality well: "'The mountains may depart and the hills be removed, but my steadfast love shall not depart from you, and my covenant of peace shall not be removed,' says the LORD, who has compassion on you." We can trust God to fulfill his promises to us, because he is the faithful Creator.

Personal Implications

Take time to reflect on the implications of Jeremiah 30:1–33:26 for your own life today. Consider what you have learned that might lead you to praise God, repent of sin, and trust in his gracious promises. Make notes below on the personal implications for your walk with the Lord of the (1) *Gospel Glimpses*, (2) *Whole-Bible Connections*, (3) *Theological Soundings*, and (4) this passage as a whole.

1. Gospel Glimpses

2. Whole-Bible Connections

3. Theological Soundings

4. Jeremiah 30:1–33:26

> ## As You Finish This Unit . . .

Take a moment now to ask for the Lord's blessing and help as you continue in this study of Jeremiah. And take a moment also to look back through this unit of study, to reflect on some key things that the Lord may be teaching you—and perhaps to highlight and underline these things to review again in the future.

Definitions

[1] **Passover** – The annual festival that commemorated God's final plague upon the Egyptians, resulting in Israel's release from Egypt.

[2] **Impute/imputation** – To attribute something to someone or credit it to his or her account. Often refers to God's crediting to every believer the righteousness of Jesus Christ.

WEEK 8:
GOD JUDGES JUDAH,
PART 1: THE LAST
DAYS OF JUDAH

Jeremiah 34:1–39:18

▲

Having stirred the hope of his readers that God will one day establish a new covenant through a Davidic king (Jer. 30:1–33:26), Jeremiah now turns to the impending judgment on Judah (34:1–45:5). This first section (34:1–39:18) recounts the final days of the southern kingdom of Judah and its destruction by Babylon in 586 BC. God contrasts his faithfulness with Judah's unfaithfulness (34:1–35:19), demonstrated in Judah's rejection of God's word (36:1–32). Instead of leading to repentance, King Zedekiah's desperation leads him to imprison Jeremiah (37:1–38:28). When at last Jerusalem is destroyed (39:1–10), Jeremiah is released (39:11–18).

The Big Picture

Jeremiah 34:1–39:18 makes clear that God is faithful to judge his people when they persistently reject his word.

> ### Reflection and Discussion

Read the entire text for this week's study, Jeremiah 34:1–39:18. Then review the following questions concerning this section of Jeremiah and write your notes on them. (For further background, see the *ESV Study Bible*, pages 1436–1444; available online at esv.org.)

1. God's Faithfulness and Judah's Infidelity (34:1–35:19)

As Jeremiah 34 opens, the Babylonian invasion of Judah is in full force, with only a few cities left unconquered (587 BC). God sends the prophet to warn King Zedekiah that he will not escape from the Babylonians; although he will not die by the sword, he will be taken captive to Babylon (34:1–7). How do King Zedekiah and the people of Judah respond to this message (34:8–16)? (For further background, see Ex. 21:2 and Deut. 15:12.) What is God's response when Judah returns to its old ways (34:17–22)?

As an expression of the covenant Judah made with God, the leaders cut a calf in half and walk between the two parts (34:18). What does this symbolic act mean? Compare this event to Genesis 15:9–20. What is the significance of the fact that in Genesis 15:9–20 only God walks between the animal pieces?

In Jeremiah 35 the scene shifts back to the reign of King Jehoiakim (609–598 BC). The prophet is sent to bring the Rechabites, a nomadic tribe descended from the Kenites (Judg. 4:11; 1 Sam. 15:6; 1 Chron. 2:55), to the house of the

Lord. During the reign of King Jehu of Israel (841–814/813 BC), Jehonadab (also spelled Jonadab) the son of Rechab helped purge the northern kingdom of Israel of wicked King Ahab's descendants (2 Kings 10:15–17). When Jeremiah offers the Rechabites wine, why do they refuse to drink it? (Consider their response in light of Num. 6:1–4.)

What lesson does Yahweh teach based on the Rechabites' obedience to their ancestor Jonadab (Jer. 35:12–18)? What does he promise the Rechabites in light of their obedience?

2. Judah Rejects God's Word (36:1–32)

To demonstrate Judah's disregard for the word of the Lord, Jeremiah recounts an event from 605 BC, during the reign of Jehoiakim. God instructs Jeremiah to have his scribe, Baruch, write down his prophecies and read them to the people in the hope that they will repent (Jer. 36:1–8). How do the people and the officials respond to the reading of God's word (vv. 9–19)?

When the scroll containing God's words through Jeremiah is read to the king, what is his shocking response (vv. 20–26)? What does God promise to do to Jehoiakim for his disregard for God's word?

Although we might not tear out pages from our Bibles, what are some ways we show a dismissive attitude toward God's Word?

---

3. Judah's Last Days (37:1–39:18)

In Jeremiah 37–39 the prophet is finally ready to recount the events surrounding the destruction of Jerusalem in 586 BC. When the Babylonians withdraw from Jerusalem to engage the Egyptian army (588 BC), Jeremiah warns King Zedekiah that Babylon will return to destroy Jerusalem (37:1–10). During this reprieve Jeremiah leaves Jerusalem for his hometown but is arrested as a deserter (37:11–21). He is thrown into a cistern and left to die (38:1–6), but Ebed-melech (whose name means "servant of the king") rescues him and moves him to the court of the guard (38:7–13). Despite a final warning from Jeremiah (38:14–28), Jerusalem is destroyed and King Zedekiah is captured (39:1–10). Jeremiah is vindicated and given the choice of either going into exile or remaining in the land (39:11–18). In what ways is Jeremiah's experience similar to that of Joseph (Genesis 37–50) and Daniel (Dan. 6:1–28)?

Compare this pattern with Jesus' experience in Matthew 26–28. How do individuals like Joseph, Daniel, and Jeremiah point forward to Christ?

How is Jeremiah's vindication a fulfillment of God's promises to him in 1:18–19?

Read through the following three sections on *Gospel Glimpses*, *Whole-Bible Connections*, and *Theological Soundings*. Then take time to consider the *Personal Implications* these sections may have for you.

Gospel Glimpses

GENUINE REPENTANCE.[1] When faced with impending disaster, the people of Judah "repented" of their sin (Jer. 34:8–10). But once the danger of judgment appeared to be past, the people returned to their old ways (vv. 11–16). The opening words of Jesus' public ministry were, "The time is fulfilled, and the kingdom of God is at hand; repent and believe in the gospel" (Mark 1:15). But as Martin Luther rightly noted, "The entire life of believers is to be one of repentance." Genuine repentance is rooted in godly sorrow that grieves over offending a holy God (2 Cor. 7:5–13). It is a gift that God gives (2 Tim. 2:25), yet at the same time it is something we are responsible to practice (Rom. 2:4).

Whole-Bible Connections

A RIGHTEOUS SUFFERER VINDICATED. As a proclaimer of God's word, Jeremiah was unjustly persecuted and thrown into a pit, yet eventually he was vindicated. His experience was part of a pattern in redemptive history of righteous sufferers, including people like Joseph before him (Genesis 37–50) and Daniel after him (Dan. 6:1–28). This pattern of a righteous man suffering, being thrown into a pit or something equivalent, and eventually being vindicated culminates in Jesus Christ. He was the embodiment of righteousness (1 Cor. 1:30), yet he suffered the greatest act of injustice in history (Matt. 27:32–54). He was put into the grave (Matt. 27:57–61) yet rose triumphant three days later (Matt. 28:1–10).

Theological Soundings

COVENANT. As part of their covenant with the Lord, the leaders of Judah cut a calf in half and walked between the parts (Jer. 34:18). By doing so they were in effect saying, "May we become like this animal [i.e., "May we die"] if we fail to keep this covenant." The Lord used this same symbolic act when he made his covenant with Abraham in Genesis 15. God promised him descendants more numerous than the stars of the sky, and Abraham believed him (Gen. 15:1–6). In the covenant ceremony that followed, only the Lord walked between the pieces (Gen. 15:7–20). By doing so God took full responsibility for fulfilling the obligations of his covenant with Abraham. He did so by taking on flesh to become the promised descendant of Abraham, who inherits the blessings promised to Abraham (Gal. 3:6–5:1). Everything that God requires for his fulfillment of his covenant, he has provided through the faithfulness of his Son, Jesus.

GOD BLESSES FAITHFULNESS. God draws a lesson on faithfulness for his people from the obedience of the Rechabites to their father Jonadab (Jer. 35:1–19). As the one who revealed himself as "merciful and gracious, slow to anger, and abounding in steadfast love and faithfulness" (Ex. 34:6), God blesses the faithfulness of his people (Gen. 22:15–18; Num. 12:7; Neh. 9:8; Heb. 3:5; Rev. 2:10). According to Jesus, faithfulness in small things is the foundation of faithfulness in bigger things (Luke 16:10–12). Jesus promises that God will reward his faithful servants on the last day (Matt. 24:45–25:46). Our faithfulness to God is rooted in the fact that Jesus Christ was "faithful over God's house as a son" (Heb. 3:6), thus opening the door to our exercise of a faith that saves; faithfulness is also mentioned as one of the fruits of the Holy Spirit's work in our lives (Gal. 5:22–23).

THE WORD OF GOD ENDURES FOREVER. King Jehoiakim thought he could disregard God's word by simply cutting it up and tossing it into the fire (Jer. 36:20–26). He learned the hard way that "The grass withers, the flower fades, but the word of our God will stand forever" (Isa. 40:8). The psalmist strikes a similar note when he writes, "Forever, O LORD, your word is firmly fixed in the heavens" (Ps. 119:89). According to Jesus, "Until heaven and earth pass away, not an iota, not a dot, will pass from the Law until all is accomplished" (Matt. 5:18). Jesus says something similar regarding his own words: "Heaven and earth will pass away, but my words will not pass away" (Matt. 24:35). Not only were heaven and earth created by the word of God, but the new heavens and new earth will also be brought into existence by God's word (2 Pet. 3:6–7).

▶ Personal Implications

Take time to reflect on the implications of Jeremiah 34:1–39:18 for your own life today. Consider what you have learned that might lead you to praise God, repent of sin, and trust in his gracious promises. Make notes below on the personal implications for your walk with the Lord of the (1) *Gospel Glimpses*, (2) *Whole-Bible Connections*, (3) *Theological Soundings*, and (4) this passage as a whole.

1. Gospel Glimpses

2. Whole-Bible Connections

3. Theological Soundings

4. Jeremiah 34:1–39:18

As You Finish This Unit . . .

Take a moment now to ask for the Lord's blessing and help as you continue in this study of Jeremiah. And take a moment also to look back through this unit of study, to reflect on some key things that the Lord may be teaching you—and perhaps to highlight and underline these things to review again in the future.

Definition

[1] **Repentance** – A complete change of heart and mind regarding one's overall attitude toward God or one's individual actions. True regeneration and conversion is always accompanied by repentance.

WEEK 9:
GOD JUDGES JUDAH,
PART 2: THE FIRST
DAYS OF EXILE

Jeremiah 40:1–45:5

▲

The Place of the Passage

Jeremiah 40–45 recounts the aftermath of the destruction of Jerusalem in 586 BC. While most residents were taken to exile in Babylon, some (mostly the poorest of the people) were left behind to scratch out an existence as best they could. Rather than submit to their Babylonian rulers, however, those who remained in Judah rebelled (Jer. 40:1–41:18). As their rebellion leads them to seek refuge in Egypt, God makes it clear that the people are rebelling ultimately against him (42:1–45:5).

The Big Picture

Jeremiah 40–45 shows us that a heart of rebellion can survive even catastrophic consequences and will eventually resurface, unless God's grace overcomes it.

> ## Reflection and Discussion

Read through the complete text for this study, Jeremiah 40:1–45:5. Then review the questions below concerning this section of Jeremiah and write your notes on them. (For further background, see the *ESV Study Bible*, pages 1444–1451; available online at esv.org.)

1. Judah's Futile Rebellion against Babylon (40:1–41:18)

Despite Nebuchadnezzar's command that Jeremiah be treated kindly (Jer. 39:11–12), the prophet is apparently caught up with the exiles taken in chains to Ramah (a small town five miles north of Jerusalem) on their way to Babylon (40:1–6). What choice does the captain of the guard give Jeremiah, and why is he given this choice? What does Jeremiah decide to do?

The Babylonians appoint Gedaliah as governor of those remaining in the land. What instructions does Gedaliah give to the people (40:7–12)? What is the significance of gathering wine, summer fruits, and oil?

What concerns does Johanan raise to Gedaliah (40:13–16)? How does Gedaliah respond?

Johanan's worst fears are realized when Ishmael and his men assassinate Gedaliah, his attendants, and the Babylonian soldiers with him (41:1–3). After disposing of the bodies, Ishmael takes the remaining people at Mizpah captive and sets out toward Ammon (41:4–10). How does Johanan respond (41:11–18)? What do the people fear will happen to them?

2. Judah's Futile Rebellion against God (42:1–45:5)

At this point Jeremiah reappears in the narrative, apparently caught up in the group of people captured by Ishmael and rescued by Johanan. What does Johanan ask Jeremiah to do (42:1–6)? How do the people promise to respond to Jeremiah's instruction?

Ten days later Jeremiah summons the people to hear the word of the Lord. What is God's message (42:7–22)? What promises and warnings does he give?

Despite their earlier promise to "obey the voice of the LORD our God . . . that it may be well with us" (42:6), the people disregard the word of the Lord and head for Egypt (43:1–7). When they arrive at the city of Tahpanhes, God once again speaks to the people (43:8–13). What is his message?

Sometime later the Lord speaks to all the Judean exiles living in Egypt (44:1–14). What practices of these exiles does God condemn? What reminders does he give? What will be the fate of those who remain in Egypt?

How do the people respond to God's message through Jeremiah (44:15–19)? What do the people resolve to continue to do?

What does this section (44:1–30) teach us about the nature and effects of idolatry? How have you seen these effects in your own life?

Read through the following three sections on *Gospel Glimpses, Whole-Bible Connections*, and *Theological Soundings*. Then take time to consider the *Personal Implications* these sections may have for you.

Gospel Glimpses

GOD IS WITH US TO SAVE US. God promises those left behind in the land that if they remain in Judah, "I am with you, to save you and to deliver you" (42:11). This promise is a picture of what God has done for us in Jesus Christ. The angel told Joseph that his soon-to-be-wife Mary "will bear a son, and you shall call his name Jesus, for he will save his people from their sins" (Matt. 1:21). Matthew explains that Jesus' birth fulfills the promises of Isaiah 7:14: "'Behold, the virgin shall conceive and bear a son, and they shall call his name Immanuel' (which means, God with us)" (Matt. 1:23). Through his death and resurrection Jesus has already saved us from our sins, and he is with us "always, to the end of the age" (Matt. 28:20) as we proclaim the good news concerning him to the ends of the earth.

GOD SHOWS ABUNDANT MERCY.[1] The people plead for mercy from the Lord (Jer. 42:2), knowing it is their only hope. Our only hope as sinners is the cry of the tax collector, who prayed, "God, be merciful to me, a sinner!" (Luke 18:13). Thankfully, God has revealed himself as "The LORD, the LORD, a God merciful and gracious, slow to anger, and abounding in steadfast love and faithfulness" (Ex. 34:6). Because God is rich in mercy, "even when we were dead in our trespasses, [God] made us alive together with Christ—by grace you have been saved—and raised us up with him and seated us with him in the heavenly places in Christ Jesus" (Eph. 2:4–6). Because we have Jesus as our great high priest, we can "with confidence draw near to the throne of grace, that we may receive mercy and find grace to help in time of need" (Heb. 4:16).

Whole-Bible Connections

GOD'S SERVANT. In announcing his future judgment on Egypt, God refers to Nebuchadnezzar as "my servant" (Jer. 43:10). Throughout redemptive history God designates as his "servant" key figures in his unfolding plan, including Abraham (Gen. 26:24), Moses (Ex. 14:31; Num. 12:7), Joshua (Josh. 24:29), David (Psalm 18 title; Ezek. 34:23–24; 37:24–25), and the suffering servant (Isa. 52:13–53:12). Each of these servants in some fashion points forward to the ultimate servant, Jesus Christ, who "emptied himself, by taking the form of a servant, being born in the likeness of men. And being found in human form, he humbled himself by becoming obedient to the point of death, even death on a cross" (Phil. 2:7–8).

FLEEING FROM GOD. When confronted with a clear word from God to remain in the land, the Jews remaining in the land chose to disobey and flee from God instead (Jer. 43:1–7). They were like the prophet Jonah before them, who, when commanded to "Arise, go to Nineveh, that great city, and call out against it, for their evil has come up before me," instead "rose to flee to Tarshish from the presence of the LORD" (Jonah 1:2–3). As Jonah learned, however, it is impossible to flee from the presence of the Lord. David affirms this in Psalm 139:7 when he asks, "Where shall I go from your Spirit? Or where shall I flee from your presence?" God made this same point to Jeremiah when he confronted the false prophets of his day: "Can a man hide himself in secret places so that I cannot see him? declares the LORD. Do I not fill heaven and earth? declares the LORD" (Jer. 23:24). Fleeing from the omnipresent² one who fills heaven and earth is an exercise in futility.

Theological Soundings

GOD RELENTS. To reassure the people that God intends to "build you up and not pull you down . . . [to] plant you, and not pluck you up" (compare Jer. 1:10), the Lord says, "I relent of the disaster I did to you" (42:10). God had repeatedly called his people to repent, promising that if they did so he would relent from bringing judgment, yet they refused. Here in 42:10 God indicates he is finished pouring out his judgment on Jerusalem, and expresses his sorrow that his people's sins have led to judgment.

GOD'S NAME. When the exiles living in Egypt resolve to continue in their idolatry, God says, "Behold, I have sworn by my great name, says the LORD, that my name shall no more be invoked by the mouth of any man of Judah in all the land of Egypt" (44:26). God's name is more than a moniker or label; it reveals who he truly is. When Moses asks God to show him his glory, God responds by passing before him and proclaiming "the name of the LORD": "The LORD, the LORD, a God merciful and gracious, slow to anger, and abounding in steadfast love and faithfulness'" (Ex. 34:5–6). The name "LORD" is inseparably tied to God redeeming his people and establishing a covenant with them (Ex. 3:13–15).

GOD'S WORD MUST TRUMP OUR CIRCUMSTANCES. God's people must constantly consider what they are allowing to define their reality: God's word, or their circumstances? Despite God's clear message to stay in the land and his promise of blessing if they did so, the people could not get past their fear of the king of Babylon (Jer. 42:1–43:7). As the one who spoke all things into existence (Genesis 1), God is the one who defines what is truly real and what is not.

> ## Personal Implications

Take time to reflect on the implications of Jeremiah 40:1–45:5 for your own life today. Consider what you have learned that might lead you to praise God, repent of sin, and trust in his gracious promises. Make notes below on the personal implications for your walk with the Lord of the (1) *Gospel Glimpses*, (2) *Whole-Bible Connections*, (3) *Theological Soundings*, and (4) this passage as a whole.

1. Gospel Glimpses

2. Whole-Bible Connections

3. Theological Soundings

4. Jeremiah 40:1–45:5

As You Finish This Unit . . .

Take a moment now to ask for the Lord's blessing and help as you continue in this study of Jeremiah. And take a moment also to look back through this unit of study, to reflect on some key things that the Lord may be teaching you—and perhaps to highlight and underline these things to review again in the future.

Definitions

[1] **Mercy** – Compassion and kindness toward someone experiencing hardship, sometimes even when such suffering results from the person's own sin or foolishness. God displays mercy toward his people, and they, in turn, are called to display mercy toward others (Luke 6:36).

[2] **Omnipresence** – An attribute of God that describes his presence in all places at all times.

Week 10: God's Judgment on the Nations

Jeremiah 46:1–51:64

The Place of the Passage

When God called Jeremiah to be a prophet, he said, "I have set you this day over nations and over kingdoms, to pluck up and to break down, to destroy and to overthrow, to build and to plant" (Jer. 1:10). To this point in Jeremiah the focus has been on God's bringing judgment on his idolatrous people while still promising future redemption through a descendant of David who would establish a new covenant. In Jeremiah 46–51, the focus shifts to God promising judgment on the nations surrounding Judah. The Lord is making it clear that he is not merely the God of Judah, but the God of the nations as well.

The Big Picture

In Jeremiah 46–51, God displays his sovereignty by vowing to judge the nations while also promising to redeem a remnant from among them.

Reflection and Discussion

Read through the complete passage for this study, Jeremiah 46:1–51:64. Then review the questions below and record your notes and reflections on this section of Jeremiah's prophecy. (For further background, see the *ESV Study Bible*, pages 1451–1472; available online at esv.org.)

1. God Will Judge Egypt (46:1–28)

The people who remained in Judah decided to flee to Egypt after Gedaliah, the Babylonian-appointed governor, was murdered. God had warned the people through Jeremiah not to seek refuge in Egypt, and here in Jeremiah 46:1–28 his reason becomes clear: just as he brought judgment on Judah, he will judge Egypt as well. The first taste of this came in 605 BC, when Nebuchadnezzar defeated Pharaoh Neco on the banks of the Euphrates (46:1–12). What imagery is used to portray Babylon and Egypt? What specific reason does God give for judging Egypt?

Judgment on Egypt will not be limited to the banks of the Euphrates; it will come to the land of Egypt as well (46:13–28). In addition to Pharaoh and the people of Egypt, who else is the target of God's judgment? How is this similar to what God did in the exodus? (Hint: look at Ex. 12:12.) What distinction does God make between his people and the Egyptians (46:27–28)?

2. God Will Judge the Philistines (47:1–7)

The Philistines were a thorn in Israel's side from her earliest days. What were some prior conflicts between Israel and the Philistines (Judg. 13:1–7; 1 Sam. 17:1–58)? What does God promise to do to the Philistines (Jer. 47:1–7)? Who/what will be his instrument?

3. God Will Judge Moab (48:1–47)

The Moabites were descendants of Lot through one of his daughters (Gen. 19:30–38). They opposed Israel in the wilderness (Numbers 22–24), and God specifically prohibited them from ever entering his assembly (Deut. 23:3). According to Jeremiah 48:1–10, in what did Moab trust for their security?

Worship of Chemosh, the chief god of the Moabites, involved human sacrifice (2 Kings 3:27). What does God promise to do to the Moabites and Chemosh (Jer. 48:11–20)? Is there any hope for the Moabites? If so, what and when? (Hint: look at 48:47.)

4. God Will Judge Many Nations (49:1–39)

In Jeremiah 49 God announces judgment on a series of nations: Ammon (49:1–6), Edom (vv. 7–22), Damascus (vv. 23–27), Kedar and Hazor (vv. 28–33), and Elam (vv. 34–39). Using the study notes in the *ESV Study Bible* (or other resources you may have), write down any interesting things you learn about these various peoples.

Which of these peoples does God promise to restore? What does this promise of restoration for Gentile peoples tell us about the character of God and his plan for this world?

5. God Will Judge Babylon (50:1–51:64)

Even though Babylon was God's instrument of judgment on Judah, the Lord makes it clear that Babylon will also be judged. What specific reasons does God give for judging Babylon? (See especially 50:2, 17–18, 29–38; 51:24–26, 47, 52–53.)

When judgment is discussed, salvation is also often promised. What will happen to the people of Israel and Judah when God brings judgment on Babylon (see 50:4–10, 17–20)? How and when will this happen?

_____

_____

_____

_____

_____

_____

_____

Read through the following three sections on *Gospel Glimpses*, *Whole-Bible Connections*, and *Theological Soundings*. Then take time to consider the *Personal Implications* these sections may have for you.

Gospel Glimpses

SALVATION THROUGH JUDGMENT. Throughout Jeremiah, God has promised not merely judgment but also salvation for his people. Judah's salvation would come, but only through judgment. This is how God always brings salvation. As Christians, the judgment we deserve for our sinful rebellion against a holy[1] God has been experienced by Jesus on the cross (Matt. 27:32–54; Rom. 3:21–26). Three days later he rose from the dead, defeating sin, death, and the Devil (Matt. 28:1–20; Col. 2:13–15). By faith we are united to Christ, sharing in his death and resurrection to new life (Rom. 6:1–11). *Our* salvation has come through *his* judgment.

FULL PARDON OF SIN. The Old Testament sacrificial system was never designed to take away sin once and for all, but rather to point forward to the one who would do so (Heb. 9:1–28). Echoing the promise of the new covenant (Jer. 31:31–34), God promises the remnant that iniquity will no longer be found among them, because of the everlasting covenant he will establish (50:4–5, 20). As believers, we have already experienced the complete forgiveness of our sins, because Jesus "has appeared once for all at the end of the ages to put away sin by the sacrifice of himself" (Heb. 9:26). When Jesus cried out from the cross, "It is finished" (John 19:30), he was declaring that he had successfully accomplished the salvation of his people, including complete and final pardon of our sin.

Whole-Bible Connections

SALVATION OF THE GENTILES. Judgment is not God's only message for the nations; several times in Jeremiah 46–51 he promises restoration as well. From the beginning, God's plan of salvation included the Gentiles. He promised Abraham that "in you all the families of the earth shall be blessed" (Gen. 12:3). As the promised descendant of Abraham, Jesus Christ is the fulfillment of this promise. Through faith in him, both Jews and Gentiles inherit the blessing promised to Abraham and are filled with God's Spirit (Gal. 3:6–29). This is the good news we are called to proclaim to all the nations (Matt. 28:18–20; Acts 1:8). We do this in anticipation of the day when there will be "a great multitude that no one could number, from every nation, from all tribes and peoples and languages, standing before the throne and before the Lamb, clothed in white robes, with palm branches in their hands, and crying out with a loud voice, 'Salvation belongs to our God who sits on the throne, and to the Lamb!'" (Rev. 7:9–10).

GOD'S JUDGMENT ON BABYLON. Later biblical authors saw in God's promise of judgment on Babylon (described in Jeremiah 50–51) a picture of God's final judgment on *all* his enemies. Already in Isaiah 13:1–22, the description of Babylon and its king transcends the earthly kingdom of the Chaldeans and represents *all* the kingdoms of this world in rebellion against God. The apostle John picks up this language in Revelation to personify[2] the coalition of Satan and the kingdoms of this world who actively oppose Christ and his kingdom. Babylon is the "mother of prostitutes and of earth's abominations" (Rev. 17:5), who "made all nations drink the wine of the passion of her sexual immorality" (Rev. 14:8). She is the great prostitute, "drunk with the blood of the saints, the blood of the martyrs of Jesus" (Rev. 17:6). When describing Babylon's ultimate destruction, John echoes the language of Jeremiah 50–51 at several points (Rev. 18:1–24), culminating in a call to "Rejoice over her, O heaven, and you saints and apostles and prophets, for God has given judgment for you against her!" (Rev. 18:20).

Theological Soundings

THE DAY OF THE LORD. Jeremiah 46:10 is one of several places in this section connecting God's judgment on various nations to the day of the Lord: "That day is the day of the Lord GOD of hosts, a day of vengeance, to avenge himself on his foes." Throughout the Bible the day of the Lord is the appointed time when God will bring about judgment on his enemies and salvation for his people (Joel 2:28–3:3). Often the day of the Lord is described in a way that both refers to the impending judgment on a specific city, nation, or people and anticipates the final judgment that will come on all creation at the end of human history (Zeph. 1:2–18). The New Testament describes both the crucifixion of Jesus (Matt. 27:45–54) and the day of Pentecost (Acts 2:1–41) with the imagery of the day of the Lord.

GOD AS CREATOR AND JUDGE. In announcing judgment on Babylon, God reminds us that his authority to judge is rooted in his identity as "he who made the earth by his power, who established the world by his wisdom, and by his understanding stretched out the heavens" (Jer. 51:15; compare 10:12–16). Similar language is found in Psalm 135:7, linked to God's judgment on Egypt and the nations defeated by Israel in the wilderness (Ps. 135:8–12). As our Maker, God has both the power and the authority to render judgment on us, and each one of us must appear before him to give an account of his or her life (Rom. 2:1–11; Heb. 9:27–28).

Personal Implications

Take time to reflect on the implications of Jeremiah 46:1–51:64 for your own life today. Consider what you have learned that might lead you to praise God, repent of sin, and trust in his gracious promises. Make notes below on the personal implications for your walk with the Lord of the (1) *Gospel Glimpses*, (2) *Whole-Bible Connections*, (3) *Theological Soundings*, and (4) this passage as a whole.

1. Gospel Glimpses

2. Whole-Bible Connections

3. Theological Soundings

4. Jeremiah 46:1–51:64

> ### As You Finish This Unit . . .

Take a moment now to ask for the Lord's blessing and help as you continue in this study of Jeremiah. And take a moment also to look back through this unit of study, to reflect on some key things that the Lord may be teaching you—and perhaps to highlight and underline these things to review again in the future.

Definitions

[1] **Holy/holiness** – A quality possessed by something or someone set apart for purposes defined by God and involving some form of purity. When applied to God himself, the word refers to his utter perfection and complete transcendence over creation. God's people are called to imitate his holiness (Lev. 19:2), which means seeing themselves as set apart from sin and reserved for obedience and service to him.

[2] **Personify/personification** – A rhetorical device attributing human characteristics to nonhuman things such as animals, plants, or objects. An example is Isaiah 55:12: "The mountains and the hills before you shall break forth into singing, and all the trees of the field shall clap their hands."

WEEK 11: CONCLUSION: THE FALL OF JERUSALEM

Jeremiah 52:1–34

The Place of the Passage

In this final chapter of Jeremiah the prophet recounts the fall of Jerusalem at the hands of the Babylonians. He begins by describing Nebuchadnezzar's siege and his eventual capture of King Zedekiah (Jer. 52:1–11). Jeremiah then turns his attention to the destruction of the temple (vv. 12–23) and the exiling of the people to Babylon (vv. 24–30). He concludes by noting that although the people are in exile, the Davidic line remains alive (vv. 31–34). Although Jeremiah has already described the destruction of Jerusalem in chapter 39, here he repeats much of that material (with some slight variations) to demonstrate that God had followed through on his repeated warnings of judgment for Judah's idolatry. Yet judgment is not the final word; as stated, the Davidic line remains alive.

The Big Picture

Jeremiah 52:1–34 shows us that God fulfills his promise of judgment on his people while keeping his promise of future salvation through a descendant of David.

> ### Reflection and Discussion

Read through Jeremiah 52:1–34, the passage for this week's study. Then review the following questions, taking notes on this final chapter of Jeremiah's prophecy. (For further background, see the *ESV Study Bible*, pages 1472–1474; available online at esv.org.)

1. Jerusalem's Fall and Zedekiah's Blinding (52:1–11)

After reminding the reader of Zedekiah's family and reign (Jer. 52:1), Jeremiah notes that "He did what was evil in the sight of the LORD, according to all that Jehoiakim had done" (v. 2). Read Jeremiah 22:13–17. What did Jehoiakim do that angered God?

The idolatry and wickedness of Judah became so bad that God "cast them out from his presence" (52:3). How is this similar to what God did to Adam and Eve in the garden of Eden (Gen. 3:1–24)?

The Babylonian siege of Jerusalem lasted 18 months. Sometime after the food ran out, the men of war breached the wall and fled south. What do the Babylonians do when they finally capture King Zedekiah (52:8–11)?

2. The Destruction of the Temple (52:12–23)

Although the Babylonians previously left Jerusalem largely intact after defeating Judah (605 and 597 BC), this time they have had enough. What does Babylonian commander Nebuzaradan do when he enters the city (52:12–16)?

Jeremiah gives a lengthy description of what the Babylonians take from the temple (52:17–23). What do the Babylonians take? Why do you think Jeremiah devotes so much attention to this?

3. The Exiling of the People (52:24–30)

This section describes groups of people either executed (52:24–27) or taken into exile (vv. 28–30) by the Babylonians. Who were the various groups of people executed? Why do you think these people were killed rather than taken into exile?

4. The Continuation of the Davidic Lineage (52:31–34)

These final verses of Jeremiah fast-forward about 25 years to 562 BC. By this time King Jehoiachin (598–597 BC) had been imprisoned in Babylon for 37 years. What does Evil-merodach, king of Babylon, do for him at this point?

Compare what Evil-merodach does for Jehoiachin with what David does for Mephibosheth in 2 Samuel 9:1–13. How are these two events similar? How are they different?

Jehoiachin was also known by another name: Jeconiah. Why is it significant that he is part of the line of David? (Hint: look at 2 Sam. 7:12–16; Jer. 23:5–6; 30:8–9; 33:14–26; Matt. 1:11.)

What is the significance of Jeremiah ending his book this way? What message is he communicating to his reader by noting that Jehoiachin was released from prison?

Read through the following three sections on *Gospel Glimpses, Whole-Bible Connections*, and *Theological Soundings*. Then take time to consider the *Personal Implications* these sections may have for you.

Gospel Glimpses

FREEDOM FROM A GREATER CAPTIVITY. After 37 years in a Babylonian prison, Jehoiachin was released and given a seat at the king's table. Imagine the joy and relief he experienced! As believers we have been set free from an even greater captivity—slavery to sin and the fear of death (Heb. 2:14–15). Because we are united to Christ by faith, we share in his death, burial, and resurrection to new life (Rom. 6:7–8). Death no longer has dominion over Jesus, so it no longer has dominion over us, either (Rom. 6:9–10). "Thanks be to God, that you who were once slaves of sin have become obedient from the heart to the standard of teaching to which you were committed" (Rom. 6:17). How much joy we should experience in light of our greater freedom!

HOPE. Amid judgment, hope remained for God's people: the Davidic line was still alive. As believers, our hope is anchored in the fulfillment of that same promise. Jesus is the Son of David who, through his death and resurrection, has begun to reign over his new covenant people (Matt. 4:17; Acts 2:22–36; Rom. 1:1–4). One day his kingdom will be visible and universal. It is "in this hope we were saved. Now hope that is seen is not hope. For who hopes for what he sees? But if we hope for what we do not see, we wait for it with patience" (Rom. 8:24–25). Before we knew Christ, we had "no hope and [were] without God in the world. But now in Christ Jesus you who once were far off have been brought near by the blood of Christ" (Eph. 2:12–13), whose kingdom will never be overthrown.

Whole-Bible Connections

THE PROMISE MADE TO DAVID. In 2 Samuel 7:12–16 God promised David a descendant who would rule over an eternal kingdom. Through Jeremiah God reiterated this promise, swearing to "raise up for David a righteous Branch, and he shall reign as king and deal wisely, and shall execute justice and righteousness in the land" (Jer. 23:5). The New Testament makes it clear that Jesus is this promised Son of David (Matt. 1:1). People desperate for Jesus' miraculous healing cried out to him as the Son of David (Matt. 9:27; 15:22; 20:30–31), and the crowds praised him as the Son of David when he entered Jerusalem the week of his crucifixion (Matt. 21:9). As the promised descendant of David, Jesus has ascended into heaven, where he sits at the right hand of God the Father (Acts 2:22–36) until the day he returns in glory with his angels (Mark 8:38).

THE TEMPLE.[1] From the beginning of creation God intended to dwell with his people. When he made the heavens and earth, he established the garden of Eden as his earthly sanctuary to dwell with Adam and Eve. But when they rebelled, God expelled them from Eden and placed angelic guards to prevent Adam and Eve from reentering (Gen. 3:22–24). God was "with" various individuals, such as Abraham (Gen. 21:22), Isaac (Gen. 26:3, 24), Joseph (Gen. 48:21), and Moses (Ex. 3:12), but it was not until the building of the tabernacle[2] that God designated a place to dwell with his people Israel (Exodus 35–40). Centuries later Solomon built the temple as a more permanent place for God to dwell (1 Kings 5–8). When the Babylonians destroyed the temple, it was natural to question whether God would ever again dwell with his people. But under the leadership of Zerubbabel and Jeshua, the exiles who returned to the land rebuilt the temple (Ezra 3–6). The Lord promised Zerubbabel that the "latter glory of this house shall be greater than the former" (Hag. 2:9). That promise was fulfilled when "the Word became flesh and dwelt among us, and we have seen his glory, glory as of the only Son from the Father, full of grace and truth" (John 1:14). Jesus is the true temple, the place where God dwells with his people (John 2:19–22). All who are joined to him by faith "are being built together into a dwelling place for God by the Spirit" (Eph. 2:22).

Theological Soundings

GRACE. Grace is God's unmerited favor shown to us. Not only did we do nothing to deserve such kindness; we did everything to deserve the exact opposite: condemnation. When Evil-merodach "graciously freed Jehoiachin . . . and brought him out of prison" . . . and "spoke kindly to him and gave him a seat above the seats of the kings who were with him in Babylon" (Jer. 52:31–32), it was a picture of God's grace to his people. Because of our sin, we deserve God's condemnation, but "God, being rich in mercy, because of the great love with which he loved us, even when we were dead in our trespasses, made us alive together with Christ—by grace you have been saved—and raised us up with him and seated us with him in the heavenly places in Christ Jesus, so that in the coming ages he might show the immeasurable riches of his grace in kindness toward us in Christ Jesus" (Eph. 2:4–7).

EXILE. Because God is holy, sinful human beings cannot enter his presence. So when Adam and Eve sinned, God sent them into exile away from his presence (Gen. 3:22–24). God had promised Israel that if they persisted in their idolatry, he would expel them from the land (Lev. 26:27–39; Deut. 28:64–68). The New Testament picks up this idea and applies it to all humanity. Paul writes that "now in Christ Jesus you who once were far off have been brought near by the blood of Christ" (Eph. 2:13). Hebrews 13:12 notes that "Jesus also suffered outside the gate in order to sanctify the people through his own blood." In his death Jesus has experienced exile on our behalf so that all who are joined to him by faith may be brought near to God.

Personal Implications

Take time to reflect on the implications of Jeremiah 52:1–34 for your own life today. Consider what you have learned that might lead you to praise God, repent of sin, and trust in his gracious promises. Make notes below on the personal implications for your walk with the Lord of the (1) *Gospel Glimpses*, (2) *Whole-Bible Connections*, (3) *Theological Soundings*, and (4) this passage as a whole.

1. Gospel Glimpses

2. Whole-Bible Connections

3. Theological Soundings

4. Jeremiah 52:1–34

> ## As You Finish This Unit . . .

Take a moment now to ask for the Lord's blessing and help as you continue in this study of Jeremiah. And take a moment also to look back through this unit of study, to reflect on some key things that the Lord may be teaching you—and perhaps to highlight and underline these things to review again in the future.

Definitions

[1] **Temple** – A place set aside as holy because of God's presence there. Solomon built the first temple of the Lord in Jerusalem, to replace the portable tabernacle. This temple was later destroyed by the Babylonians, rebuilt, and destroyed again by the Romans.

[2] **Tabernacle** – The tent where God dwelled on earth and communed with his people as Israel's divine king. Also referred to as the "tent of meeting" (Lev. 1:5). The temple in Jerusalem later replaced it.

WEEK 12: SUMMARY AND CONCLUSION

▲

We will end our journey through Jeremiah by summarizing the big picture of God's message through Jeremiah as a whole. Then we will consider several questions in order to reflect on various Gospel Glimpses, Whole-Bible Connections, and Theological Soundings from the entire book.

The Big Picture of Jeremiah

Before Jeremiah was even born, God appointed him to be "a prophet to the nations" (Jer. 1:5). He put his words in Jeremiah's mouth and set him "over nations and over kingdoms, to pluck up and to break down, to destroy and to overthrow, to build and to plant" (v. 10). Even though Jeremiah ministered in a time and place very different from today, his words were "written for our instruction, that through endurance and through the encouragement of the Scriptures we might have hope" (Rom. 15:4). As believers there is much we can learn from Jeremiah, so it is important to grasp the big picture of the book.

After the opening chapter describes Jeremiah's call, God charges his people with covenant adultery (Jer. 2:1–6:30) and exposes their idolatry (7:1–10:25). Instead of remaining faithful to the Lord their husband, Judah chased after false gods while retaining the outward appearance of devotion to the Lord. But God is not fooled, and he repeatedly warns that he will send Judah into exile for its persistent rebellion. As both spurned husband and sovereign judge, God has the right and authority to hold his people accountable for breaking his covenant.

Most of the people do not appreciate God's words spoken through Jeremiah, and they take their anger and frustration out on the prophet. Jeremiah encounters repeated opposition and wrestles with his seemingly impossible calling (11:1–20:18). His confrontations with Judah's people, false beliefs, kings, and false prophets put Jeremiah's life in constant danger (21:1–29:32). Amid his suffering, however, Jeremiah experiences an even deeper relationship with God.

Despite the heavy emphasis on judgment throughout the book, Jeremiah 30:1–33:26 describes the glorious promise of future redemption. God will restore his people to the land and establish a new covenant with them. Through a descendant of David, God will rule over his people in righteousness, do away with their sin, and write his law on their hearts. As believers, we participate in that new covenant through the finished work of Jesus Christ.

Yet before the new covenant can come, judgment must fall on Judah (34:1–45:5), on the nations (46:1–51:64), and on Jerusalem itself (52:1–34). But even amid judgment, God promises to bring restoration not only to his people but to the nations as well.

Gospel Glimpses

As we have worked our way through Jeremiah, we have seen numerous glimpses of the good news of God's promises to his people. Jeremiah shows us the richness of the gospel from various angles and perspectives. Take time to reflect on the different ways you have seen the "immeasurable riches of his grace in kindness toward us in Christ Jesus" (Eph. 2:7).

What are some specific ways Jeremiah has brought new clarity to your understanding of the gospel?

What particular passages or themes in Jeremiah have led you to a fresh understanding or a deeper grasp of God's grace to us through Jesus?

Whole-Bible Connections

Jeremiah is a crossroads of a number of important themes running from Genesis to Revelation. Take some time to reflect on the various connections you have seen through your study of Jeremiah.

How has your study of Jeremiah filled out your understanding of the biblical storyline of redemption?

What themes from Jeremiah have deepened your grasp of the Bible's unity?

What passages or themes have expanded your understanding of the salvation Jesus accomplished for us? What specific aspects of Jesus life, ministry, death, or resurrection have you seen in a fresh light?

What connections between Jeremiah and the New Testament were new to you?

Theological Soundings

Jeremiah has much to teach us about what we should believe as Christians. Numerous doctrines and themes are developed, clarified, and reinforced throughout the book, such as the character of God, the sinfulness of humanity, the identity of the Messiah, and the restoration of God's people.

Has your theology shifted in minor or major ways during this study of Jeremiah? How so?

How has your understanding of the nature and character of God been deepened by this study?

What unique contributions does Jeremiah make toward our understanding of Jesus' character and accomplishments in his life, death, and resurrection?

What, specifically, does Jeremiah teach us about the human condition and our need for redemption?

Personal Implications

God gave the book of Jeremiah to transform our lives. As you reflect on the book of Jeremiah as a whole, what implications do you see for your own life?

What implications for life flow from your reflections on the questions already asked in this week's study concerning Gospel Glimpses, Whole-Bible Connections, and Theological Soundings?

What have you learned in Jeremiah that should lead you to praise God, turn away from sin, and trust more firmly in his promises?

▶ As You Finish Studying Jeremiah . . .

We rejoice with you as you finish studying the book of Jeremiah! May this study become part of your Christian walk of faith, day by day and week by week throughout all your life. Now we would greatly encourage you to study the Word of God on a week-by-week basis. To continue your study of the Bible, we would encourage you to consider other books in the *Knowing the Bible* series, and to visit www.knowingthebibleseries.org.

Lastly, take a moment to look back through this study. Review the notes that you have written, and the things that you have highlighted or underlined. Reflect again on the key themes that the Lord has been teaching you about himself and about his Word. May these things become a treasure for you throughout your life—this we pray in the name of the Father, and the Son, and the Holy Spirit. Amen.